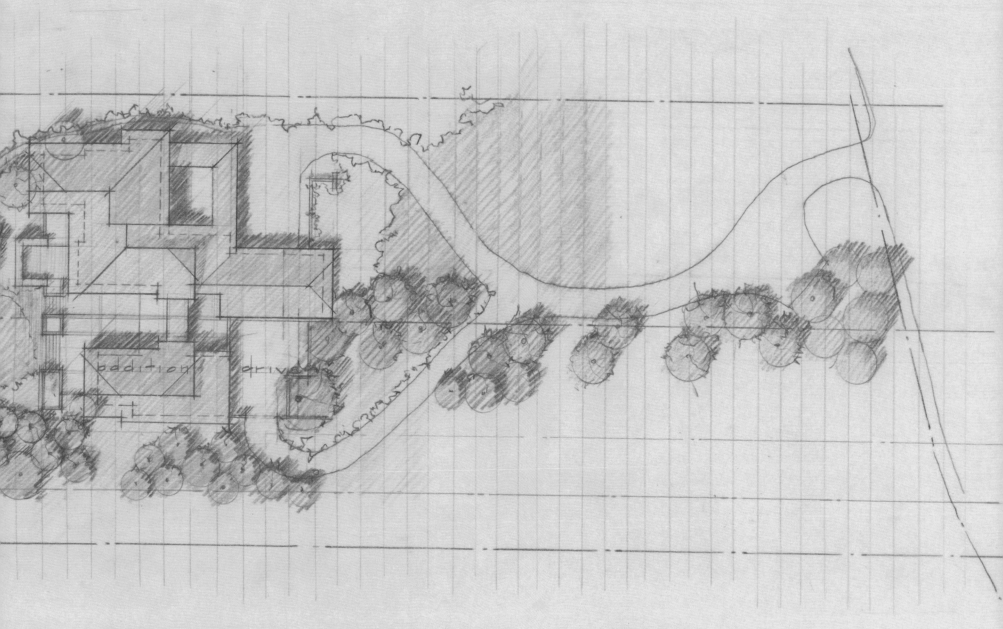

addition   driveway

GORDON WALKER

GORDON WALKER

A POETIC ARCHITECTURE

Grant Hildebrand

ARCADE, SEATTLE

These, Gordon's friends,
holding in highest regard and affection
Gordon's work and GORDON himself,
have given their abilities
to the making of this book:

GRANT HILDEBRAND

BRENDAN CONNOLLY

DAVID GOLDBERG

WILLIAM HOOK

JEFFREY MURDOCK

KELLY RODRIGUEZ

ANDREW VAN LEEUWEN

A prolific and talented architect, Gordon Walker has charmed an extraordinary number of clients and repeat clients—from California to Seattle to Idaho—with a creative modernism that is friendly to site, climate, context, culture, and the people lucky enough to know this delightful person.

Douglas Kelbaugh FAIA
Emil Lorch Professor of Architecture, Dean Emeritus
Taubman College of Architecture and Urban Planning
University of Michigan

THIS BOOK IS DEDICATED TO
ALENE MORIS AND FLOYD UDELL JONES
WHOSE GRACIOUS GENEROSITY
HAS MADE IT POSSIBLE

CONTENTS

	ACKNOWLEDGMENTS	8
	PREFACE	9
	INTRODUCTION	11
1	A HOUSE FOR THE RAFFS	13
2	GORDON'S EARLY YEARS	31
3	OLSON/WALKER 1970–78	47
4	OLSON/WALKER 1978–85	63
5	GORDON, 1985–90	75
6	WALKER ARCHITECTURE	85
7	GORDON AT MITHUN	115
8	A PREFAB ON ORCAS ISLAND	127
9	TEACHER AND MENTOR	141
10	HORSE	149
11	A POETIC ARCHITECTURE	151
12	COGNATE THOUGHTS	155
	NOTES	156
	TIMELINE	158
	DRAWINGS	165
	INDEX	180
	BIBLIOGRAPHY	182
	AUTHOR BIOGRAPHY	183

ACKNOWLEDGMENTS

MOST BOOKS ARISE FROM THE CONTRIBUTIONS of many people. That is especially true of this book: From the outset it has engaged the efforts of a team. Kelly Rodriguez, who has been the foundation and the superstructure of the serial *ARCADE*, has kept notes, read texts, refreshed memories, raised money, and served as liaison with the designer and publisher. Bill Hook was part of the Olson/Walker firm for many years, as architect and as an extraordinary graphic artist. In recent years he has turned his talents to painting as fine art, for which he has received significant recognition, but for this book he most kindly returned to his graphic talents. Andrew van Leeuwen, architect and for many years one of Gordon's closest friends, contributed his distinctive professional photographic skills. Architect Jeffrey Murdock is the only PhD among us. He has done research for almost every chapter, he wrote the earliest drafts of chapters 3 and 4, and chapter 12 is entirely his. Brendan Connolly is a partner in Seattle's renowned Mithun firm; David Goldberg is its president. They enthusiastically prepared the essay on Gordon's role with the firm, and provided a wealth of images. To say that I could not have completed this book without the contributions of these people is not a cliché. Each shares my belief in the worth of Gordon's story. I am so very grateful to them all.

The publication of this book also depended on the many who contributed to its costs; they are listed on page 184. I thank them all. Alene Moris and Floyd Jones were extraordinary in their generosity; the book is dedicated to them. Gordon and Peter Miller augmented my thanks to Alene and Floyd by preparing for them a grandly creative lunch not soon to be forgotten.

Nor could I have managed without the help of my wife, Miriam. She has helped me with many books; I think her interest in this one is special. She has patiently served as sounding board, critiquing, challenging, suggesting, weighing ideas, over hundreds of lingering breakfasts.

I intended from the outset that this be a book whose quality would reflect that of its subject. With that in mind, I sought the production services of Ed Marquand's team and facilities. Adrian Lucia of Lucia|Marquand accepted the project with an enthusiasm that proved to be unwavering. I was lucky in that, and lucky too that Ryan Polich accepted the challenge of designing the book; his work speaks for itself, eloquently. I thank them both.

Given the expertise and dedication of these many contributors, there is no way to avoid the conclusion that the book's faults must be assigned to me.

GH

PREFACE

Poiesis: to bring into being what has not previously existed.

THERE IS A POETICS TO ARCHITECTURE. It is specific and undefinable. No one speaks of it, yet it is literal and, in certain light, obvious.

It is, of course, not necessary. A building will stand perfectly well with not a poetic note to its soul. It may reproduce, it may flourish, and it may even be loved. For all of the extraordinary new diagnostics and software, there is not a single false boast claiming to meet with poetics.

Nor is it a value, at least in measurable terms, as sustainability, or durability, or even responsibility might give a stronger breath to a building. It is a known, a proper and un-numbered fact, and it is structural, in the sense of the strength and confidence that it supports.

For many people, poetics is not the reason they go into architecture. And for some, it is precisely the reason they go into architecture. But it is a pale siren, poetics, and poorly nourished and often away and never of any help with the real work of a day. It is hard to find, if ever to find, hard to trust, and heartbreakingly fragile, when you could use its comfort.

To have it, you must not have it. It is not an ally, holding up one end while you get the other end in place. No, it is a sense and a taste or perhaps a tincture. And it is absolute—you shall have none of it without the commission of all of you. Those are the terms and those are the terms.

You shall give all of yourself and still you might not get even a whiff. But you stay at it for you know the whiff and the terms. And going back on them is a kind of debt.

Poetics is, by its elusive DNA, exactly fair. Given its conditions, one could grumble that it can afford to be fair.

There are people who leave architecture specifically because of poetics—not the labors of it but the realization that it has no vote, it has no chair, it has no enforceable force. It has honor and no legal support; it is a single mark. It is a dream and a dare.

And yet, it is poetics that silently protects all of architecture. The task of architecture is to do it well—it is poetics that makes the task so difficult, so agonizing, so consumptive, so obvious.

These are clever times—you can buy the clothing of poetics, but for the body and the soul of it, you can only do the work and hope and try. And believe.

This is a book about Gordon Walker and his work as an architect. He rarely will speak about poetics, but it is always there. It is the reason Grant Hildebrand knew that he would write this book and give this book its life. You do the work, and hope and try. And believe.

Peter Miller

INTRODUCTION

THIS BOOK BEGINS WITH A PROJECT Gordon Walker designed, and in some degree built, three years after he left college. Only in chapter 2 does the story turn to his birth and early life, his college years, his marriage, and his coming to Seattle. This is an odd way to tell a story. But Gordon's career is little known outside the profession, and even within it, so I thought it would be helpful, even necessary, to present an example of his work at the outset.

Although Gordon's work is centered in the Puget Sound region, it can be found from San Diego to the Canadian border. He has designed over thirty residences, several of them built with his own hands, a host of buildings and master plans for universities throughout the Northwest and California, three buildings for the Pacific Northwest Ballet, myriad commercial buildings, and a wine bar. Likewise, the scale of his projects ranges widely, from a bird feeder to academic campuses. Thus the narrative cannot describe the continuous development of a type, as is possible for, for example, the houses of Frank Lloyd Wright's Prairie School era. Although Gordon's projects will be shown to have certain common threads, this story must describe the qualities of his work in terms of individual designs, emphasizing their particular strengths. I discuss here in some depth thirty-one of Gordon's projects that I believe convey the range and quality of his work. This story must also tell something of Gordon's teaching, for he has been a prolific educator and mentor, at the universities of Idaho and Washington and, for fifteen years, at Mithun, one of the nation's finest architectural firms, where mentoring is a specified part of his role.

And a caveat: Gordon's life has been a complicated one, and this narrative must be, at times, complicated as well. I ask the reader to be patient.

In my early college years I happened on Bruno Zevi's *Architecture as Space*. Until that encounter I had thought of architecture as object,

as solids—columns, walls, pediments, buttresses. Zevi's book opened a door for me. It led, over time, to a view of architecture as experience. To this was added, in 1978, an interest in concepts that had their beginning in the work of Jay Appleton.[1] I presented my view of the concepts, and my development of them as they applied to architecture, in two books, of which *Origins of Architectural Pleasure*,[2] and particularly the idea of complex order, are germane here. I believe the idea is a useful means for understanding Gordon's work, and as such it is a theme of this book.

In architectural literature the word "project" is often used to identify a commission that remains unbuilt. I use the word here less specifically, to refer to any architectural design; its fate, whether unbuilt, built and existing, built and altered, or built and demolished, is described in the text or captions. The term Puget Sound School used herein is my own. It refers to that body of wooden architecture that flourished in the Puget Sound region from 1951 through the mid-1970s; its patriarch was Paul Hayden Kirk; Ralph Anderson was its most prolific practitioner.

Gordon was cofounder of the esteemed Olson/Walker firm. He was retained by the University of California for planning and building designs for its Irvine, Davis, Riverside, and San Diego campuses, and the University of Idaho for its Moscow campus. The nationally renowned NBBJ firm sought him out for their staff, as did nationally renowned Mithun. Much-honored Wendell Lovett, FAIA, needing help with the finest commission of his career, turned to Gordon.[3] So did distinguished interior designer Jean Jongeward, for the finest commission of her career. Many of Gordon's clients, residential and otherwise, returned to him for a second and third project; many became his friends over the decades. Yet, with a modesty that is almost self-effacement, he evaluates his career as "above average." That is true, of course, but this book will show that he understates the case.

1 A HOUSE FOR THE RAFFS

IN 1965 KATHERINE AND DOUGLASS RAFF bought a lot on Comstock Street on Seattle's Queen Anne Hill. The lot was on the south side of the street, sloping down from the sidewalk, with a view to the Seattle Center and the Alki Peninsula beyond. Twenty years earlier, in World War II, the lot had been a "victory garden," a pear tree orchard with vegetables planted between the trees. A few of the orchard's trees remained, including, near the sidewalk, an example whose structure would grow to magnificence. In 1966, having thought about the site for the better part of a year, Kathie and Doug asked Gordon Walker to design a house for it. Kathie remembers the occasion:

> We didn't interview, we didn't shop around, we just asked Gordon. We felt we were embarking on a special project; we were young and ready for adventure. We got together and began talking, and the more we talked the more excited we became. We had a sense that Gordon had worked with some of Seattle's most highly regarded architects and was on his way to a distinguished career. Part of this came to us by the way Gordon talked, a whole new vocabulary and understanding, and his ability to visualize in three dimensions and actually sketch (and later draw plans) in three dimensions. It was a whole new and exciting experience for us, and we were too young and naïve to think of any reason why we shouldn't do this.[4]

The Raffs had met Gordon a year earlier; mutual friends had invited them to view a speculative house Gordon and Jim Olson had designed and built in the Mount Baker neighborhood. Kathie and Gordon's wife, Bobbie, had developed a friendship, and Doug and Gordon also found much in common; Gordon said, "Our chemistry clicked."

As Kathie said, they were young, all in their twenties. Doug had gone from Butte, Montana, to Harvard, for an undergraduate degree in 1961, and a degree in law in 1964. He and Kathie came to Seattle immediately on his graduation. He had found a position with Riddell, Williams, Voorhees, Ivie & Bullitt; he would remain with the firm throughout his active years in law. Gordon had come from Sandpoint, Idaho, and spent his college years at the University of Idaho, Bobbie at nearby Washington State. They married in their senior year, graduating in 1962, Bobbie in education, Gordon in architecture. They too came immediately to Seattle—it was the summer of the Century 21 world's fair—and it seemed the place for Gordon to begin his career. When the Raffs met him he was working part-time for Ralph Anderson. Anderson was one of that notable group of architects, defined by their ubiquitous and elegant use of wood, that flourished in the Puget Sound region from 1951 to the mid-1970s; they might properly be called the Puget Sound School. Paul Hayden Kirk was its patriarch; Anderson was an almost equally important figure, and its most prolific practitioner (1.1). Gordon admired both.

But by 1966 wood of high quality was less abundant and more expensive, and Gordon had heroes other than Anderson and Kirk. "My fascination with Louis Kahn never ventured very far from my thoughts."[5] Gordon especially admired Kahn's Trenton, New Jersey, bath houses: four pavilions, square in plan, in a cruciform grouping, each with a pyramidal wooden roof of shallow slope over bold, even monumental piers of exposed concrete block. Gordon thought concrete might be worth trying for the Raff design: "The idea was inspiring to me." He described the idea to Kathie and Doug, they endorsed it with enthusiasm, and the decision was made. Gordon wanted concrete block masonry rather than poured or precast concrete, for practical, aesthetic, and historic reasons: it would require no costly formwork; "the horizontal and vertical modules would contribute a personal scale"; and Gordon had in mind both Kahn's Trenton buildings and Frank Lloyd Wright's California patterned concrete block houses of the 1920s. In supporting the decision, the Raffs were adventurous, even brave. In a neighborhood of traditional homes of quality, a house of exposed concrete block was likely to meet with mixed reviews.

1.1 Ralph Anderson, the Bellevue Clinic, Bellevue, Washington, 1967–68. Designed just after Gordon left Ralph's office, it is typical of the work done during Gordon's tenure, and typical too of the quality of wooden architecture in the region at that time. Photograph by AKS Architecture.

1.2 Gordon Walker, the Katherine and Douglass Raff house, Seattle, WA, 1966; contract drawing, plans sheet.

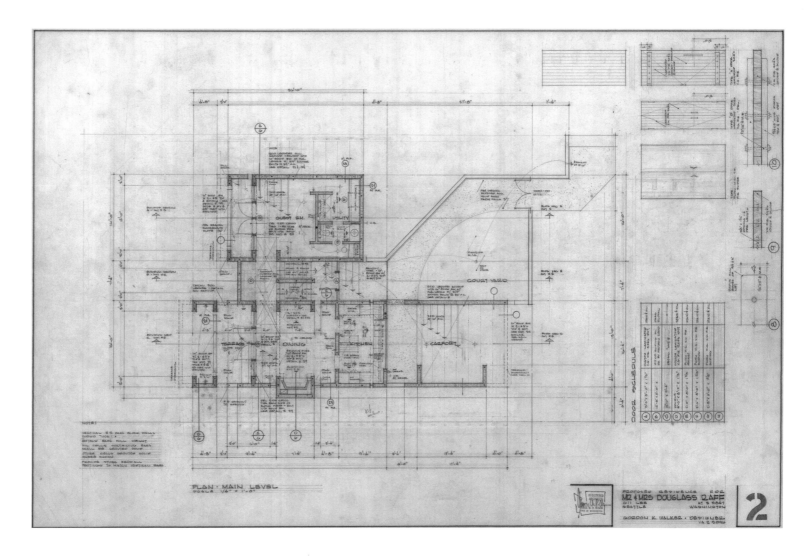

PLAN · MAIN LEVEL

A HOUSE FOR THE RAFFS

Doug Raff's avocation was books, to read, to collect, to possess, so the house must be a container for books, a live-in bookcase. He already had a sizable library, much of it on law, of course, but a good bit too on history, and architecture, and maps: he had begun to build a collection of antique maps. Kathie was equally well read, and very architecturally aware. For her, dining was the time of being together; the house must make dining a special occasion. And although the Raffs would achieve a handsome income and a reassuring wealth over the years, the budget for the house was meager.

There are seven large sheets of contract drawings for the house, drawn entirely by Gordon's hand. They are complete and impressive, in organization, line weight, poché, and lettering. They portray a design for a house that is small, and extremely complex.

The basic organization is easy to describe: A central stair is flanked on either side by a three-story volume; forward of the larger, eastern volume, and aligned with it, is a one-car carport (1.2). The elevations are more complicated (1.3). They describe a strong sculptural exterior form, and suggest interior complexities, which are clarified by the section (1.4, 1.5). The ground floor of the eastern volume is a "game room." On the floor above are a kitchen and the dining space that is the heart of the entire design (1.6). It rises through two stories; its fireplace and bookshelves are seen from the kitchen to the north, and from the living space, which is felt to be a balcony, on the floor above to the south. The western volume is simpler. The lowest level is a children's sleeping and play space, the middle level is a guest room; the top level, opposite the living space, is the master bedroom.

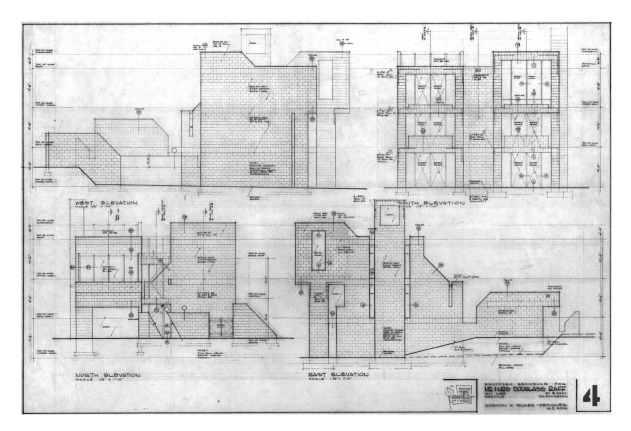

1.3 The Raff house; contract drawing, elevations sheet.

1.4 The Raff house; contract drawing, sections sheet.

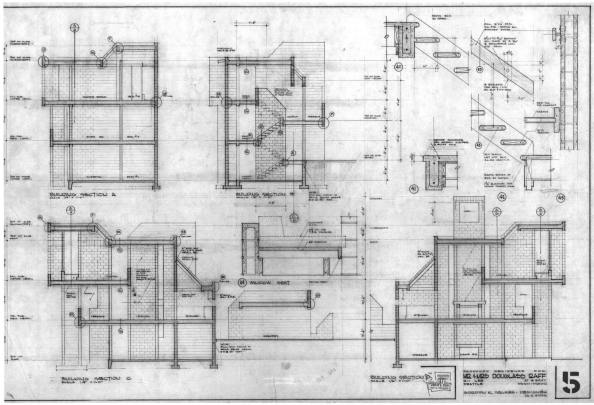

1.5 The Raff house: (top) diagrammatic plan; (center) section; (bottom) east elevation; drawings illustrating the orderly but complex organization of the design, emphasizing the wing walls. At top: The plan below the stair, symmetrical about both axes, could be the plan of a Carnegie library or a university classroom building. Drawing by Bill Hook.

Gordon had done his own structural calculations before, with qualified success. This time he retained Dean Ratti as structural engineer. In addition to the usual structural considerations and provisions, Dean and Gordon devised a series of short east-west wing walls that project symmetrically but at various spacings along the north-south walls of the eastern element (1.5, 1.6). Their ostensible purpose is to resist east-west lateral—seismic—forces.

Gordon developed the design simultaneously in plan, section, and elevation, and rapidly; the design came quickly, "rather easily," he says, with few or no studies of alternative ideas. This quick development of a single idea was unlike that of almost any other architect including Ralph Anderson for whom Gordon was working; evaluation of all reasonable alternatives is a fundamental canon of a design process. But Gordon could evaluate a number of alternatives mentally, rapidly, without drawing any option other than the one he believed to be the right direction. This highly unusual ability to settle very quickly on an optimal scheme would be a defining characteristic of Gordon's entire career.

Finding a builder became an unanticipated problem: none was to be had. Residential builders thought the design was too unusual, too unlike the typical wooden Northwest house. For larger contractors it was too small, too intricate, not worth their time. Gordon was forced to realize, "If I wanted this house built, I'd have to do it myself." He acted as his own contractor, securing subcontractors for electrical work, plumbing, heating, roofing, poured concrete, and cabinetry. He found an experienced mason for the block walls, and a skilled carpenter for the work entailing wood. He did with his own hands all he was capable of doing well.

Building a concrete block wall demands skill, care, and experience. Verticality must be continually checked, as must the horizontality of ascending courses; vertical joints must align as the courses ascend; steel reinforcing bars must be placed. Gordon helped to place them, and carried the hod with supplies of blocks and mortar, but the mason did the actual laying of the blocks.

1.6 The Raff house; an isometric drawing emphasizing the wing walls that establish order and complexity throughout the design. Drawing by Bill Hook.

1.7 The Raff house; the site as seen from the northwest, 2017. Photograph by Andrew van Leeuwen.

Beams might have been of poured-in-place or precast reinforced concrete, or steel or wood for that matter. But Gordon wanted to maintain the block module; so the beams are made of typical blocks set vertically; "soldier coursing" is the mason's term. The top of a typical beam is in compression, which the blocks can comfortably handle. The bottom is in tension, which the blocks have almost no ability to resist; Gordon wove the necessary steel reinforcing through the blocks' lower voids.

For all the dominance of the masonry, there is a lot of wood in the design. The floors throughout are of wood joists carrying plywood subflooring; Gordon made this decision so he could build them. The Raffs had several inherited rugs they wanted to use, which led Gordon to specify oak flooring throughout. Ceilings are of re-sawn cedar; doors, door and window frames, railings, and tops of balcony half-walls are of fir; kitchen counters are oak. The carpenter directed this work where necessary, and helped with some of the labor, but Gordon provided most of it, months of it; he began to think of the house as a house of wood. He said more than once that if his car broke down—which was likely—he'd fix it with wood.

Kathie remembers that when they began the adventure, "We didn't have the good sense to design a house that would be suitable for kids. I think we assumed they'd fit in somehow when the time came." Colin was born in 1969, a few weeks before they moved into the new house. "There was no nursery, the bottom floor was unfinished, and for his first couple of years Colin slept wherever we could find room for a crib." When their second child, Katherine, came along in 1973, Gordon redesigned the bottom floor to divide it into two rooms. To maximize their necessarily small size he designed the dividing wall between them to provide for one bunk bed above the other, the wall jogging in section to assign the lower space to one room, the upper space to the other. Thus the floor area of each child's room is more than half of the footprint for both.

In the early 1980s the Raffs moved the window wall of the "game room" outward, to make its deck a part of the den's interior. The living room at the top of the house proved to be less convenient than they had foreseen, and they found themselves using the enlarged ground floor den more and more as a living room. So they soon decided to move the living room furniture to the ground floor. Thereafter it would be the living room; the space that had served that purpose became Doug's retreat. For clarity in these pages we will stay with the original designations.

The approach to the house begins at the northwestern corner of the lot, at the interesting pear tree (1.7). Even as a young tree it must have been unusually configured; its twisting trunk has grown over the years to something that might rightly be called majestic. Beyond, the walk immediately bends half-left, to a diagonal view of the house that dramatizes the tree's sculptural character (1.8). The low diagonal wall leads the eye to the entry (1.9).

1.8 The Raff house in 2017. The pear tree is supported on a column of Gordon's design. The entry is at center, the carport at left. The kitchen's skylight is left of the entry. Photograph by Andrew van Leeuwen.

One enters at the half-level, to descend or ascend to the cross-axis that accesses all spaces at either side of the stair on all levels (1.10–1.12). Downward, the den is at left, the children's room at right. Upward at left is the entry to the dining space (1.12). The underside of the living loft is close overhead, and in this lower zone the dining space is symmetrical about the fireplace centerline. But it doesn't feel symmetrical, because taken in its entirety it is decidedly not.

The fireplace and its towering bookshelves are at right, a buffet and more towering bookshelves are opposite. Both are flanked by the little wing-walls, the southern of them linked by the balcony edge of the living space above. The two-story part of the dining space, from the edge of the living "balcony" to the kitchen (1.10, 1.11), is about eleven feet across—the house is small in plan dimensions—and almost nineteen feet high. This is not only a two-story space; it is a space of extremely vertical proportion (1.13, 1.14). Kathie recalls: "In early days Doug and I would lie on the dining room floor so we could look up two stories to the cedar ceiling."

Up another two half-flights is the top of the stair; the repetitive circulation cross-axis opens at right to the master bedroom, left to the living room that hovers above the dining space (1.15, 1.16). The den, dining space, living room, children's spaces, and the master bedroom all look out to the terraces and the planting beds of the back garden (1.17).

The house has had its problems, some not very serious, some more so. In addition to the living room that needed relocating, the skylight over the master bedroom—over the bed, specifically—leaked. Kathy remembers "many nights with our bed rolled out into a safe part of the room so we could place buckets under the drips." And "many, many hours were spent on our roof, repairing leaks." These problems could be fixed, and they were: Gordon redesigned the sloping skylight as a vertical clerestory with an operable window, and for the roof the Raffs found "Anthony Paynter, who not only was the smartest roofer in the world but liked

our house and wanted it to work." The kitchen was small (1.10, 1.12), and the baths very small, but with some equipment upgrades over the years, the Raffs found them acceptable for both daily life and entertaining.

That was just as well, because those spaces could not be expanded. The children had very limited spaces: Where was Colin to build a model railroad, Katherine a dollhouse? The house has had to remain small: its exterior forms do not welcome additions, and modifying the interior spaces would be difficult indeed, defined as they are by reinforced concrete. Yet in spite of the limitations it established on the Raffs' lives, for almost five decades Kathie and Doug stayed in the house Gordon had designed for them, regretfully leaving only when, with advanced years, they were less able to manage the stairs. Kathie says:

> There are decisions one makes that have a lasting effect, even if at the time one may have been thinking only of the near future. What makes a life different? Chance, sometimes. Good luck, but you make your own luck. One of the decisions we made in our marriage that had the effect of placing us in a category of awareness that influenced almost everything that followed, was building the Queen Anne house.

Kathie wanted a dining space that would do more than accommodate daily dining and frequent entertaining—she wanted something to celebrate those events, and she got it: Gordon designed for her a space of striking, memorable drama. And although the living space as designed was awkward in its location, it fully shared that drama. Doug wanted a house that would accommodate a lot of books, and he too got what he wanted: The towering shelves in the dining space held something like eight hundred books. Young Katherine said, "The soaring bookcases gave the dining room a 'great hall' feeling." Neither she nor Colin had any say in the design, of course, but Katherine liked the house; for

1.9 The entry. Unlike others in the house, the opening is not spanned by a soldier-course beam. Photograph by Dan Farmer.

1.10 The kitchen in 2017. Photograph by Andrew van Leeuwen.

1.11 The kitchen in 2017, looking southeast toward the dining space. The living space "balcony" is visible beyond at center right. Photograph by Andrew van Leeuwen.

1.12 The dining space in 1968, on entry from the stair landing, with the kitchen at left, and a window to the garden at extreme right. A soldier-coursed beam spans the openings to the kitchen. Photograph by Dan Farmer.

1.13 The dining space in 2017, looking southwest. At right and extreme left are the shelves that, in the Raffs' days, were filled with hundreds of books. The soldier-course beam is evident. Immediately beyond, framed by the little wing walls, are the entries to this space and, above, the "balcony" of the living space. Photograph by Andrew van Leeuwen.

1.14 The dining tower, 1968. Photograph by Dan Farmer.

1.15 The Raff house, 2017, the living space looking southwest. The Alki peninsula can be seen on the horizon. At right is the passage to the master bedroom; at extreme right is the overlook to the dining space below. Photograph by Andrew van Leeuwen.

1.16 The Raff house, the living space in 1968, looking down to dining and kitchen spaces. A soldier-coursed beam spans the openings to the kitchen; the wood cap to the "balcony rail" is visible at lower right. Douglass's books tower above the fireplace. Photograph by Dan Farmer.

1.17 The Raff house, the back garden
as seen from the dining room deck.
Photograph by Andrew van Leeuwen.   27

1.18 The Raff house from the southwest. The living room with its balcony is at upper right, the master bedroom is at upper left. The children's spaces at left open to the Gordon-designed little metal balcony. Photograph by Andrew van Leeuwen.

her it was a castle. The concrete blocks were "as thick, cool, and dignified as the stone walls of a fortress." The voids at the ends of second-story porches, the living room's "balcony," and the stairwell, called to her mind "arrow slits in castle walls." Colin remembers, "The rough planes of the concrete blocks gave a suitable backdrop for my father's collection of antique maps." The house matured as Colin did: He remembers returning after a long absence to realize that "stark modernity had aged into classic modernism."

In Gordon's design it is hard to know what serves only a program function, what is purely structure, and what exists for aesthetic purpose. The towering dining space, the little wing walls, serve all three purposes inseparably, as do the soldier-coursed beams. And all of these elements comprise a highly ordered but complex composition.

The order is itself complex. As we enter the dining space we are in an asymmetrical relationship with a biaxially symmetrical space; with no scale indicated, the plan could be for a Carnegie library. When we move to the intersection of the axes, however, one axis disappears, so to speak, because the living space intrudes on the cone of vision to destroy the symmetry around the east-west axis. When we move to that living space, we find that it too is biaxially symmetrical at floor level, but nearer the ceiling it is symmetrical around only one axis. (Symmetry is a familiar characteristic in nature, to which we are sufficiently attuned that asymmetry—the lobster's one large claw, the flatfish's eyes—seizes our attention. It may be that symmetry's ubiquity in nature, including its presence in ourselves, may explain its ubiquity in renowned architectural examples. Again, we often regard its absence, asymmetry, as a puzzle, insisting that we engage it: for the first-time viewer of Chartres, the spires offer this challenge.)

Wordsworth described poetry as "similitude in dissimilitude"; John R. Platt spoke of it as "a pattern that contains the unexpected"; for Gerard Manley Hopkins a poem entailed "likeness tempered with difference." Neither difference nor dissimilitude, however, seems quite on the mark; perhaps Wordsworth, Platt, and Hopkins would accept the paraphrase that poetry can be described as complex but ordered discourse. Music, too, can be defined as complexly ordered sound. The spare phrase does no justice to the magnificent phenomenon; still, music is complexly ordered sound—ordered in Western music by both rhythm and octave, with possible polyphonic complexities that can seem astonishing. The lust for complexly ordered sound is universal: all cultures of which we have any knowledge have devised their versions of it. Longfellow said, "Music is the universal language of mankind." So too dance can be described as poetry as complexly ordered verbal discourse. And so too those many complexly ordered buildings, architecture, that have been highly valued across cultures and across time. That the Raff house, in its complex order, locates itself in this company may be one reason—perhaps—for its appeal.

The house was publicized locally, was featured in the Seattle Art Museum's 22nd Annual Exhibition of Residential Architecture, and received a 1971–1972 American Institute of Architects–Sunset Magazine Western Home Awards Citation.[6] Surprisingly, the neighborhood's residents came to accept the house quite quickly and, eventually, to take some pride in it, as a significant work of architecture that distinguishes their neighborhood.

Near the end of a day of cold, drizzling rain, the project almost complete, Gordon, drenched, is sitting on the not-quite-finished upper deck he has been working on (1.18). He is looking out to the view, and down to the city, imagining his friends—Dave Fukui, Jim Olson, Ralph Anderson, Dan Calvin, Dave Hewitt—in their warm, dry offices, while Gordon is "freezing my ass off. I've got to get myself registered, be a real architect." He was twenty-seven.

2 GORDON'S EARLY YEARS

GORDON KENDALL WALKER CAME INTO THIS WORLD on February 12, 1939, in Des Moines, Iowa, the first of four sons born to a middle-class Midwest couple. His father, Harlan Walker, was a mortician who placed a high value on aesthetics. He spent much time with the subjects of his attention, diligently preparing their appearance for open-coffin viewing, whether or not that was to be the case. He had little respect for those of his colleagues who depended on a closed coffin to conceal less meticulous work. Yet the most frequent phrase Gordon remembers hearing from his father was, "Always be useful." His mother, Margaret Louise Walker, was a beautician. As befit her vocation, she too was highly conscious of physical appearance. Gordon has no memory of preschool years, but he remembers that as he reached school age she tirelessly groomed him every morning, chose his clothing for appearance rather than durability, fussed over his haircuts. She believed, and often said, that children should be seen, not heard, and that sparing the rod would spoil the child. She acted on her beliefs: Gordon felt with some frequency the sting of a branch from a nearby tree, fetched by him for the purpose, after a major transgression, or maybe a not-so-major one.

Long before Gordon's school days, however, the family had left Iowa. With the attack on Pearl Harbor on December 7, 1941, and America's entry into the war, Harlan Walker had been assigned to the Farragut Naval Training Station on Lake Pend Oreille in northern Idaho, an hour's drive from the Canadian border. He dreamed of managing a fishing resort some day—he had a site in Wisconsin in mind—but he grew to love northern Idaho, and he began to think it might equally satisfy his dream. By war's end he had discovered, near Lake Pend Oreille, a small abandoned town called Talache (2.1), built in the 1920s by the American Tobacco Trust as a model silver-mining town. It comprised a forty-eight-room boarding house, a post office, a grocery store, an assay office, two dozen small houses, a lodge, some miscellaneous outbuildings, and 800 acres of land. The mine proper had some workshops and repair sheds, and a four-story "ball mill" for crushing the ore. Derelict though it was, Walker thought the town could have a future. He convinced his sister, brother, and another investor; they worked out the financing, and bought the town *in toto*. Lake Pend Oreille was renowned for its world-record rainbow trout;[7] Walker thought that he, his brother-in-law Wayne Anderson, and whatever other help they could find, could make Talache a destination fishing resort. Its centerpiece would be the long, low lodge. It needed work, like everything in Talache, but it included three fireplaces of handsomely laid local stone, and a sixty-foot screened porch that commanded a breathtaking view of the lake.

Gordon's experience in building began there. His father, aware of the magnitude of the task he was facing, had taken some time to learn the basics of carpentry, and talked to Gordon about it; uncle Wayne had some experience in construction, and openly shared it. Gordon listened and watched, and helped as much as a small boy could, as his father and uncle chopped brush, straightened salvaged nails, replaced rotted floor joists and flooring, strengthened roof trusses, rehung doors and repaired their hardware, patched, painted, and stained walls, ceilings, and woodwork, and repaired and installed roofing. Under his father's guidance and his uncle's tutelage, Gordon experienced every imaginable condition of construction in wood. By such means his father, his uncle, and to some extent Gordon, created a successful fishing resort. "Talache Lodge" became what Harlan Walker had hoped it would be.

As Gordon reached the age of eleven he discovered an interest in animals. He acquired four goats, and with his mother's mandates about appearance in mind, and help from his father and uncle, he remodeled a large woodshed into a goat barn. By the time he was fourteen the herd had grown to forty-five, and he had converted an old horse stable into a far larger barn. With that accomplished, he decided he had had enough of remodeling and repairing, and enough of farming too. He turned to guiding hikers and fishers, and became the youngest licensed fly-fishing guide in Idaho.

Gordon's earliest formal education was in a crossroads six miles away called Sagle—a house, a gas station, a country store, and a school. The school was in a small and otherwise vacant building: two rooms, each with a woodstove to do battle with the winters of northern Idaho. The few students were farm kids, whose attire was well-worn overalls and muddy boots; Gordon's polished shoes and pressed slacks had no chance of fitting in.

The Sagle school taught only through the sixth grade; from the seventh grade onward Gordon went to Sandpoint, whose population of 3,500 made it the second largest town in northern Idaho. The school was large enough to let a student find a niche; Gordon found several. He studied art, watercolor and drawing mostly, which he liked enormously; he learned to play the clarinet well enough to be in the school band, and he liked that too; and he played a lot of football—Sandpoint was a sports-minded town. In his senior year, 1956–57, Gordon was elected president of his class of 120 and, as winter set in, he was selected as First Team All-State center, not an easy position to play. Football notwithstanding, he had done well enough in his classes to let him think he could be admitted to a college; the high school yearbook tells us his goal was to graduate from college in architecture.

He had only a vague idea then of what architecture was, but from their stays in Talache he knew and liked several art and architecture faculty from the University of Idaho in Moscow. Knowing little about other schools—knowing little about Idaho, for that matter—Gordon applied, and was accepted for the five-year professional architectural program; few students can have entered such a program with equal experience in down-to-earth building. Somewhere along the way he met Ralph Reinhold, publisher of *Progressive Architecture*, and Reinhold gave him a subscription.

In his first year Gordon was not at all sure he had chosen the right program. He could see that architecture was something other than what he had seen done at Talache, but what that was remained unclear; "I didn't get it," he remembers. By his second year he had sorted out a working grasp of what it was all about. The culture of an architecture program at any school is shaped by

2.1 Talache, Idaho, ca. 1923; the mining town, with the resort at the lakefront. Photograph by Ross Hall.

the design studios—the casual atmosphere, the collegiality and competition of shared problems, the exhaustion of late nights and all-nighters, models and sketches everywhere, grand presentation drawings, the excitement of the jury. And when in 1926, at the age of twenty-seven, Theodore Jan Pritchard started the Department of Art and Architecture and was professor and chair, he gave real meaning to the department's title: all the visual arts, and architecture, would be taught "under a common roof"—the roof of a converted horse stable, as it turned out. (Pritchard taught in the department through 1967, chaired it for the first thirty-seven of those forty-one years, and was the dominant faculty figure for much of that time.) So Idaho's architecture studios were further enriched by the proximity, occasionally the participation, of the art students. By his second year Gordon had become totally engrossed in the culture: "I loved what I had chosen for my life's work." He started keeping a mattress under the drafting table, so he could

sleep in the studio when he worked late, or exhaustion could no longer be ignored. With due respect for his teachers, he believes he learned as much from fellow students—particularly Nels Reese, a soon to be highly regarded professor—as from the faculty.

At the beginning of his second year Gordon pledged Phi Gamma Delta. He was lonely, and fraternities offered friendships; he chose Fiji from among them in part because he thought the architecture of the house was outstanding. It had been completed in the mid-1920s, the decade when so many architecturally distinguished Greek houses were built on so many American campuses. Whitehouse and Price were architects for the Idaho house. Harold Whitehouse designed the majestic Cathedral of St. John the Evangelist that commands the hill above Spokane, and the music building at the University of Washington, but the firm's design for the Idaho fraternity is not quite of that quality. They sought to evoke an English country manor (2.2): but the right side of the entry façade is of brick from grade to gable, while the remainder of the exterior, in not too convincing half-timbering, seems to belong to a different building. Seen from the background of Sandpoint, however, and absent any immediate rivals, to Gordon the design seemed exceptional. From his second year on he worked in the kitchen in exchange for room and board. On Mondays he got to cook; he liked to do it, and he was good at it.

No more than forty feet separated the back of the house from the back of the Kappa Kappa Gamma sorority. In the morning, still more after nightfall, many Fijis payed close attention to the Kappa windows. "TV2" was the signal to the brothers that something worthwhile was in progress. Gordon mentioned to a Kappa one day that one of the sisters might put on a show some evening, with sisters stationed at adjacent windows armed with serious flashlights. The Kappa did her number, and when her program was nicely under way, the sisters illuminated the attentive faces of a lot of Fijis, several of whom were dating Kappas. This adventure illustrated another facet of Gordon's personality—for while it was

possible to be angry with him, and the brothers certainly were, it was impossible to dislike him, and the brothers didn't.

In his early years, while tending goats in the meadows outside Talache, lonely, maybe a little bit afraid, and emulating his father, Gordon began whistling. This is an entirely usual event for someone of that age in any circumstance, of course. But over time Gordon would transform this simple behavior into something that could be called serious music; in his later professional years his whistling could be mistaken for a well-played flute. He had probably come quite a way along that path in these college years.

During Gordon's second year at Idaho his parents sold Talache and bought a property in Sandpoint's Syringa Heights, on a hill overlooking Lake Pend Oreille. They had some plans and "clippings" for the house they wanted to build, and they asked Gordon to help them. The design was "early American," not Gordon's sort of thing at all, but, he said:

2.3 Ludwig Mies van der Rohe and Philip Johnson, The Seagram Building, New York City, 1958. Photograph by Andrew van Leeuwen.

2.4 Paul Hayden Kirk, the Magnolia branch of the Seattle Public Library, 1962–63. Photograph by Grant Hildebrand.

I wanted to help and to learn. So I drew the basic construction drawings, added a few twists, then helped them over that summer, starting with digging the foundations. As summer was ending I was on the roof helping lay the hand-split cedar shakes. I've never liked them, because they are laid as shingles not shakes, a big aesthetic difference. Over the next two years I was a constant consultant, and I did the exterior staining before bringing my girlfriend home to meet my parents. I fell off the ladder the day before she arrived, so I was a bit gimpy during her visit.

In the years Gordon was in school, the most influential figure by far in the realm of architecture was Mies—Ludwig Mies van der Rohe (2.3). Nearly everyone who was then or would soon be a major American figure in the profession—other than Wright, of course—designed within Mies's influence at one time or another.[8] His influence was perhaps even stronger in the schools. Few schools would have told students they must design in that way, but the better marks often tended to go to those who did. Whatever the values of Mies's influence, and they were many, the architectural philosophy was one of spare austerity: "less is more." Gordon appreciated that philosophy. But he sought a richness as well, and he found it in the architectures of other times and places; he loved the classes in architectural history. They were taught by Pritchard, the school's best lecturer, which certainly contributed to their success. What historical material did Gordon like best? "All of it."

Pritchard's lectures ended with the early twentieth century. Gordon augmented them by reading Henry-Russell Hitchcock's *In the Nature of Materials*,[9] the first critical book on an extensive selection of Frank Lloyd Wright's work. Gordon also read periodical articles on Seattle architect Paul Hayden Kirk; Gordon "thought the sun revolved around him" (2.4).

Since Idaho is a land-grant school, service in the Reserve Officers' Training Corps—ROTC—was mandatory. Training four times a week, Gordon accrued a little more than the usual number

of demerits. Forty-five or more meant a court-martial, which might mean expulsion from the corps, which would certainly mean disastrous loss of deferment. Gordon wore his uniform for work in studio, built models in it, cooked the fraternity's dinners in it. At the end of term he turned the thing in, and its condition pushed his demerits into court-martial territory. He was court-martialed—a day late; he forgot the original appointment, and was forcefully reminded. He was found guilty. He asked what he could do to make amends—and not for the first time, nor the last, luck, and charm, were in Gordon's corner. The corps had materials that needed framing. Gordon said he could do it. He had the materials framed by a professional shop for $12 each, returned them to the officers within a week. They were impressed by his speed, and still more by the caliber of his craftsmanship.

In Gordon's third year he was to be awarded the Hummel Prize, 150 meaningful dollars, for outstanding work in design. But he didn't collect the dollars: he turned in the requisite project a day late.

In his fourth year he received a fellowship to represent the department at the student American Institute of Architects (AIA) meeting in Washington, DC. Having read Hitchcock, he went by train to Chicago to spend a week looking at Wright's work. He went to the Riverside, River Forest, and Oak Park suburbs, and to the University of Chicago area to see Wright's Robie house, then almost derelict. Of the profusion of examples, Oak Park's Unity Temple (2.5) held Gordon's greatest interest—for its fusion of the massive and the delicate, its oneness of structure and form, and its articulation of what Louis Kahn, fifty-six years later, would call master and servant spaces. From Chicago he flew to DC, there to hear Kahn's familiar talk on what a brick wants to be. It brought into his experience the realization that architecture could have an intellectual dimension. When he returned to Moscow, having seen Wright's work and heard Kahn's words, he knew he had some thinking to do, and it would take a little time. He was unable to

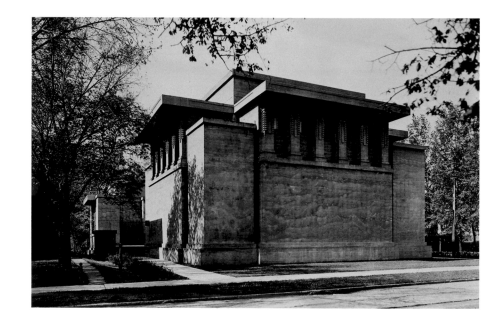

2.5 Frank Lloyd Wright, Unity Temple, Oak Park, Illinois, 1904. Gordon's admiration for this building would remain undiminished throughout his life. Photograph courtesy The Frank Lloyd Wright Foundation Archives (The Museum of Modern Art | Avery Architectural & Fine Arts Library, Columbia University, New York).

design anything for weeks. These experiences would have a life-long influence: When, in his seventies, Gordon was asked about buildings he admired, he cited Unity Temple above all others, and he was still excited by Kahn's words and work:

The next summer I designed a neighbor's house from the ground up, inspired by Wright's drawing of the John Pew house in Madison, Wisconsin, that I loved [2.6]. I spent the summer helping frame the house, once falling off the scaffolding with a wheelbarrow full of cement…big ouch! The design was compromised…a lot! This was a lesson for me in the importance of a close relationship with the client.

Gordon's senior design studio project, the only college project of which he kept a record, was a master plan for the Talache Resort, and a design for a waterfront yacht club (2.7, 2.8, 2.9). The

2.6 Frank Lloyd Wright, the John Pew house, Madison, Wisconsin, 1940; much of the drawing is in Wright's own hand. Courtesy The Frank Lloyd Wright Foundation Archives (The Museum of Modern Art | Avery Architectural & Fine Arts Library, Columbia University, New York).

yacht club is a composition of vertical slabs in a roughly triangular grouping derived from a grid. Its most dominant characteristic is the three prow-like corners, where the slabs, presumably concrete, are separated by shafts of glass. The drawings include a profusion of details, but the design itself looks hurried: 45-degree interior corners need more study; the perspective's simplicity is unconvincing. Nevertheless, the project was important to Gordon's future. In its design, for the first time, he let form be the dominant issue, regarding the building as sculpture, something more than a

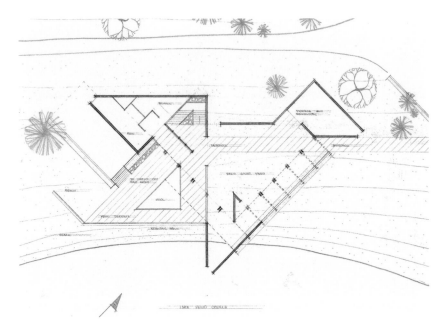

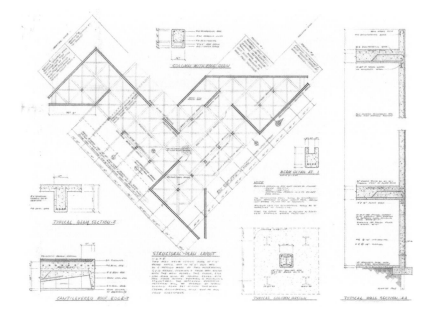

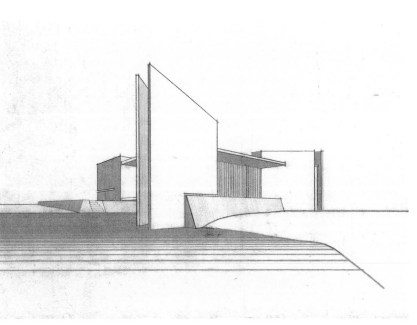

2.7 Gordon Walker, A Waterfront Yacht Club, senior project, University of Idaho, 1962; site plan.

2.8 Yacht Club; plan.

2.9 Yacht Club; perspective from the water.

workable plan with rooms properly sized. He had no critiques on the project; the teachers seemed to want him to carry it through on his own, and he did.

Idaho brought few speakers to the campus, so Gordon spent some time traveling to Boise, Seattle, Spokane, and often to Washington State University at Pullman, six miles away, which also had an architecture program. Gordon made a number of friends there, one of whom, in Gordon's fourth year, arranged a blind date. Gordon had dated a little at Idaho, including a few with a Kappa Kappa Gamma homecoming queen, but none had resulted in a serious relationship—nor did the Pullman blind date. But she introduced Gordon to a friend, Roberta Tonn, "Bobbie," a student in education at WSU. A week later Gordon asked Bobbie for a date, one date led to another, and they fell in love. At the beginning of his fifth year, her fourth, the last college year for both of them, they married—he was on time for the wedding, barely. After marriage they lived in Pullman, and he commuted to Moscow for his classes.

Gordon graduated in June of 1962 at the age of twenty-two; he was one of a class of eleven. His Bachelor of Architecture degree, B.Arch., was a professional credential that, with a three-year internship, would qualify him to sit for registration exams. Bobbie graduated from WSU the same month with a degree in education. She and Gordon immediately moved to busy and exciting Seattle; the Century 21 Exposition had opened in April. Bobbie quickly found work teaching freshman English at Highline High School. Gordon's admiration for Paul Hayden Kirk led him to apply at Kirk's office, with no success: Seattle has long had an overabundance of architects, and the fair brought many more. Gordon finally found a job with Ralph Decker, a respected and competent architect, though not one with abundant design awards.[10]

Early the next year, disenchanted with the office practice, Gordon gave his enthusiasm to painting, in the evenings, in oil—mostly abstracts, an occasional still life: he said, "Architecture, as practiced, had very little stimulating juice to it; painting did." The effort was sabbatical or escape as well as achievement. Examples ranged from adept and interesting to work Gordon thought "should have been lost at sea."

That summer, with Bobbie free from classes, Gordon left Decker's office. Having saved (almost) enough money, they took "that long-awaited trip to see the cities and buildings [of Europe]"; Gordon had dreamed of this since the days of Pritchard's classes. They took Banister Fletcher's dull but encyclopedic *History of Architecture on the Comparative Method* as a reference, and Arthur Frommer's *Europe on Five Dollars a Day*. (It could be done then if you were grimly determined, but a few more dollars, or several, here and there, were all but essential.) Through Auto Europe they bought a Citroen 2CV, the timeless Deux Chevaux, two horsepower—utterly primitive, reliable, enduring, gutless, engaging in its bare usefulness. Gordon loved it.

They began in Paris. They would try for five dollars a day by camping for most of the trip—with seats removed the floor of a Deux Chevaux could sleep two, and they had a small Coleman camp stove. But in Paris a hotel was unavoidable. Among the city's abundant riches, Gordon was most moved by the tailored lower and upper banks of the Seine, the lower and upper chambers of La Sainte Chapelle, and the park at the east end of the Île de la Cité, with the apse of Notre-Dame as background. From Paris they drove southwest to Chartres, then east to Bourges and north through Reims, Laon, Amiens, and Beauvais, a circuit of the great northern French cathedral towns. Gordon was thrilled by them all, and was most moved by the glass of Chartres and the height of Amiens.[11] He was impressed that Laon on its mesa and Mont Saint-Michel in its tidal sea were built at all. Then across the channel to London, Gordon taken by the sheer dense urbanity of the city, its warm and welcoming pubs, Westminster Abbey and Hall, and the reserved creativity of Wren's city churches.

In Denmark they traveled with Gordon's university room-mate, Carl Magnusson, "the most cosmopolitan person I had ever met," who would later be Director of Design for Knoll International. Magnusson introduced them to Arne Jacobson, Borge Mogenson, and Sigurd Lewerentz, and took them to Jorgen Bo and Wilhelm Wohlert's still little-known but exquisitely crafted Louisiana Museum of Art north of Copenhagen, which impressed Gordon immensely. With some anxiety they drove through Checkpoint Charlie to a recently walled Berlin, much of it still rubble, "a major contrast to Western culture, stark, monumental, cold, austere." Then they headed south through Tito's Yugoslavia to Athens, Olympia, and Mykonos. The rough Greek villages with their ubiquitous unfinished houses were "a real shock, poor but colorful." Having seen photos of the Acropolis from earliest school days, Gordon expected it to be boringly familiar. Not so: he was thrilled, and remained on the great white aerial plateau, the earth fallen away, for hours.

In Rome the list of things to see was long—Pantheon, Colosseum, Forum, Baths and Forum of Trajan, Baths of Caracalla, though to Gordon's great regret they missed the Caravaggios in San Luigi dei Francesi. He said, "The thing that struck me most was the in-fills over time, that make up the fabric of history." Then through Pisa, Florence, and Milan to Barcelona. Gordon would have liked to see Mies's Pavilion at the 1929 exposition grounds, but it was long gone, of course. He recalled that Antoni Gaudí's Sagrada Familia "was sitting there in a pile of weeds. No tourists, no workers, only one guard, who let us climb to the top—the inspired spires, out of this world."

While they were climbing Gaudí's spires, a local driver smashed into the passenger's side of their 2CV. It was still drivable, but "the bodywork was toast." And with ten days to go, Gordon and Bobbie were almost out of money: for two days they had been living on ears of corn picked from farmers' fields along the way.[12] Luck, Gordon's charm, and his range of talents, served them again.

They met a couple with a new VW Squareback, a brother and sister, wealthy, obviously bored with each other. They had lots of food in the car, hated to cook. Gordon said he'd be happy to do the cooking, and there it was: ten days of meal tickets. They followed the couple to share four days in Madrid, then, stopping along the way, the VW with the food, Gordon doing the cooking, they convoyed in tandem to arrive in Paris a day before their flight home. Although they had cut it very close indeed, they had diligently kept twenty dollars tucked away for a last grand Paris dinner. But Gordon's luck had run out. He had forgotten the twenty-dollar airport tax. Dinner was a shared banana.[13]

In his time with Decker Gordon he had become "enchanted with Ralph Anderson and his special brand of Northwest residential architecture." Anderson was one of that group of architects, dedicated to an architecture of wood, whose work, largely in the Puget Sound region, was of a pervasive quality unsurpassed in its time (2.10). Anderson was the most prolific figure of the group, and his work at its best was among the finest examples of the Puget Sound School, which placed it among the finest of its type anywhere. He was also a leader in the preservation of earlier architecture of quality, particularly in Seattle's Pioneer Square area. Ralph was generous, too, in giving young architects in the office freedom and responsibility,[14] often putting projects entirely in their hands; the office had a reputation as a vigorous training ground.

Gordon had sent Anderson several postcards during the trip. When he returned to Seattle he went to Anderson's office to apply for a job, and was offered one: It was "a new adventure. I wanted to design and build every day." Gordon's first assignment was the design of an exterior light fixture. Anderson couldn't understand Gordon's drawings, or pretended not to, and soon said, "Go build the thing, we'll see how it turns out." Gordon built the thing, it turned out well, and became the prototype for exterior lamps for several of Anderson's projects. As Gordon worked

2.10 Robert Chervenak (Grant, Copeland, Chervenak), Hugo Winkenwerder Hall, School of Forestry, University of Washington, 1960. In its paired beams, its cantilevered upper floor, and its pervasive use of wood including an exposed wood structure, the building is a typical example of the Puget Sound School. The building is reminiscent of Paul Kirk's office on the eastern shore of Lake Union. Photograph by Andrew van Leeuwen.

41

2.11 "The House in the Trees" and "The Children's House," 1965–67, Kirkland, Washington (radically remodeled). The main house is the larger volume at left; the bridge and the Children's House are at right. Entry is at the center of the main house. Drawing by Bill Hook.

through projects assigned to him, he quickly assimilated Ralph's way of design. It was said around the office that he could out-Ralph Ralph.

Anderson's office was on the third floor of a building he had newly acquired in Pioneer Square. When he moved into it, it was the only occupied building in the district. He rented space to other tenants, most of them in associated fields: Dick White was co-owner of the Foster-White Gallery; Bill Speidel ran the tourist-oriented "Underground Tours." Jean Jongeward, on the second floor, was an interior designer Ralph often worked with, and he had chosen her wisely. Self-trained, she was thought by many to have been the most talented of her profession in the Northwest, and unlike many in the field at the time, her work was entirely in the spirit and the substance of Ralph's architecture and that of his compatriot colleagues.[15] Gordon said:

> Jean was the one I was immediately drawn to. Architecture was BUILDINGS. Jean talked about how people _lived_ in them, furniture, materials, color; great stuff to learn at age twenty-four! She had an incredible, intuitive ability to deal with the light and color that make the Northwest special. She spent four years trying to perfect khaki. Ralph was already there—he understood materials, color, the value of detail, beyond anything I had been introduced to, and Jean added to it. She was involved in a number of his projects at that time. I was a sponge and soaked up everything they were thinking and doing. They became lifelong friends.

Gordon would have met others there as well: George Suyama, Bill Booth, Dan Calvin, Jerry Stickney, David Fukui—and Jim Olson, whose time with Anderson overlapped Gordon's years.

In 1964 daughter Meagan was born, and Gordon and Bobbie bought a lot in Kirkland, northeast of Lake Washington, a wooded steeply

sloping two-thirds of an acre, with a view of the lake. The next year Gordon reduced his hours with Anderson to half time, and borrowed $11,000 to design and build "a house in the trees" for the growing family, and a studio for his work. He hired two carpenters for two weeks to frame the house, and he hired an electrician and a plumber. The rest of the work he did himself. The largest plan element of the house was nearly symmetrical—this was to be typical of Gordon's plans—its asymmetry arising from a dramatic mansard-roofed peninsula opposite the entry (2.11). The brutally austere studio—its windows made of Visqueen rather than glass—was built for eight hundred dollars. Both buildings were nearly finished by 1967, when the second child, son Colin, was born. Gordon then added a "Children's House": a three-story tower, reached from the main house by a bridge. Gordon was not entirely satisfied with the house proper. The visual weight of its dominating mansard roof seemed contrary to the idea of a house in the trees; the skylights leaked; and Leonard, the Irish setter, "made the house shake when he ran around the deck"—this in an earthquake zone. For all its austerity Gordon liked the studio (2.12, 2.13): "It was a place to do what I loved," and the Children's House with its bridge was a delight. Unfortunately Gordon took very few photos, and most of them are compromised by the trees and heavy undergrowth.

In 1965 Gordon designed, for a site on Lake Washington, the first of three houses he would do for Jane and Pat Rogers (2.14, 2.15, 2.16). It would be one of the few of his designs, and the last, to emulate the work of Ralph Anderson. It falls solidly within the greatest years of the Puget Sound School: Chervenak's Winkenwerder building (2.10) dates from 1960; Kirk's library (2.4) is of 1962–63. Since the late 1990s the house has been owned, maintained, and cherished by Abbie and Scott Morris.

In that same year, 1965, Gordon and Jim Olson designed, and Gordon built, a speculative house in Seattle's Mount Baker neighborhood. Gordon and Jim would soon form a partnership that for fifteen years would produce work of distinction, and each of them

2.12 Gordon Walker, the Kirkland studio, 1965–67. Photograph by Gordon Walker.

2.13 Gordon Walker, the Kirkland studio, 1965; plan, sections, and elevations. Drawing by Bill Hook.

2.14 Gordon Walker, the Rogers-Morris house, Seattle, 1965: the house atop its hill. Photograph by Andrew van Leeuwen.

2.15 The Rogers-Morris house: Gordon designing within the Puget Sound School, and out-Ralphing Ralph. Photograph by Andrew van Leeuwen.

2.16 The Rogers-Morris house, the kitchen with the deck beyond, looking to Lake Washington. Photograph by Andrew van Leeuwen.

would have a subsequent individual career of equal distinction. But the Mount Baker house was not a work of distinction. In its plan organization it worked well enough, but the massing was not a success. Nevertheless, Gordon and Jim needed a buyer, and they held an open house to try to get one. Katherine and Douglass Raff came to such events, not to buy, but to experience the work of various architects, hoping to find the right one for a project of their own. They liked many things about the house, and they looked around for one of its designers. Gordon happened to be nearby, talking with Bobbie. The four of them chatted, enjoyed the conversation, agreed to meet again soon, did, and became friends. In due course the Raffs were invited to the home Gordon had designed and built in Kirkland. They liked it and they decided to tell Gordon about their project. 45

3 OLSON/WALKER 1970–78

WHEN GORDON BUILT THE SPECULATIVE HOUSE in which he first met the Raffs, he and Jim Olson were sharing a small office in Seattle's Mount Baker neighborhood. In 1967 they moved their still separate practices to a space in the architect-filled third floor of the Maud Building in Pioneer Square, near Ralph Anderson's office. Anderson had thirty houses on the drawing boards at the time, much more than he could do. He fed some of the work to Gordon, who thereby found himself with a burgeoning practice.

One element of that practice was a house on Mercer Island for Mr. and Mrs. William Waddington (3.1). The Raff house is a study in masonry; the Waddington house develops the same general plan—a central stair with a three-story volume to either side (3.2)—as a study in wood. Gordon saw it as an homage to the heavy-timber-framed stables and barns of his Talache days. Spatially the interior repeats the idea of a loft, in this case for sleeping, that overlooks the tall dining and living space. The structural elements, all of them exposed on the interior and inboard of the wall surfaces, are organized into a geometric order, and the points of connection and intersection are beautifully thought through (3.3, 3.4). But the formal order of the little Raff wing walls is absent in the Waddington design, while its lateral rigidity depends on diagonal framing and wall sheathing, so the simpler exterior lacks the Raff's cantilevers, shadowed recesses, and generous sweeps of glass.

In 1969 Gordon was approached by Peter Kunstadter, a research professor at the University of Washington, to design a house for him and his wife, an artist. They had seen the Raff house and were attracted to it; they wanted a bunker, something of concrete and steel. In 1953 Kunstadter's parents had commissioned the modernist firm of Keck and Keck to build a house of steel and glass in the Highland Park suburb of Chicago. The house had won an AIA award; the younger Kunstadters also wanted a house of significance. Their site, on Bellevue's Evergreen Point, was steeply sloped, dropping away to a Lake Washington waterfront. Gordon quickly provided a conceptual design. It was a cousin to the Raff design, 47

3.1 Gordon Walker, the William Waddington house, Mercer Island, Washington, 1968. Photograph by Dick Busher.

3.2 Gordon Walker, the William Waddington house, Mercer Island, Washington, 1968. Diagrammatic drawing by Bill Hook.

though a distant one, with a much more pronounced asymmetry, and massive intersecting concrete walls that tied the house to the steep site, with double cantilevers to create decks and habitable spaces. But the estimates came in too high, again, and as he had done with the Raff project, Gordon decided to build the house largely by himself, acting as general contractor, mason, carpenter, and cabinetmaker.

Gordon's career had been and would be one of excellent buildings and happy clients. The Kunstadter house (3.5–3.7) has since been demolished, and only one barely publishable photo exists. The design is again a fascinating example of order and complexity, as Gordon's plan and the diagrammatic drawing by Bill Hook reveal. But this was not a story of happy clients. They lived in Hawaii during construction, returning to Bellevue only when the house was nearly finished. It was not at all what they wanted, nor thought they were getting, although Gordon had been closely in touch with them at all stages of the work. They sued Gordon for a long list of what they identified as defects. Gordon agreed that there were technical errors, and corrected many of the problems, and the parties settled. But Gordon was deeply shaken by the experience, and shortly thereafter was in the hospital with stomach ulcers. This was the sixth and last project in which he would act as designer-builder.

Gordon and Jim had become close friends. Jim had signed Gordon's drawings for the Raff house; he drove out to Kirkland several times to see Gordon's progress on his house in the trees and, later, the children's tower and its bridge. Jim and his wife, Katherine, and Gordon and Bobbie spent occasional long evenings over one of Gordon's dinners, sometimes the four of them, sometimes with other friends. It seemed only natural, even inevitable, that they would associate in some formal way, and they did. They both wanted to address work of a larger scale, and they created Architectural Design Associates to seek that kind of work. But the firm remained only a name, and was soon abandoned. Instead, in

3.3 The Waddington house, the sitting space, with exposed structure that is typical throughout the design. At all connections the timbers bypass one another, a detail that is structurally sound, constructionally straightforward, and aesthetically expressive. Photograph by Dick Busher.

3.4 The Waddington house, three sections. All roof rafters and diagonal bracing elements are at the same angle. This order is exploited to create spaces of quite different configurations. Drawing by Bill Hook.

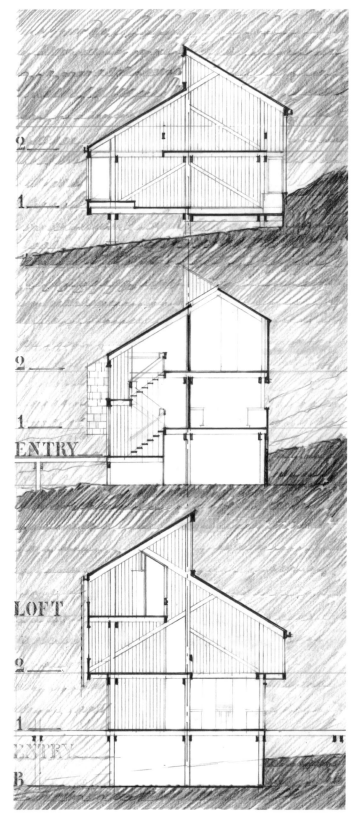

3.5 The Kunstadter house, 1970.
Concrete block revisited. Biaxial
organization but without symmetry, an order that is itself complex.
Diagrammatic drawing by Bill Hook.

3.6 Gordon Walker, the Peter Kunstadter house, Bellevue, Washington, 1970 (demolished). Photograph by Gordon Walker.

3.7 The Kunstadter house, the plan as drawn by Gordon, in 2018, from memory.

1970, Jim and Gordon formed a partnership that would practice for the next fifteen years as Olson/Walker. It was a decision that would have a large impact on the architectural quality of Seattle and the region.

Early days of the partnership were much as they had been: each partner brought individual commissions into the office, each partner remained in charge of his own projects. Among those on Gordon's drawing board in 1971 was one that was not his own, which deserves mention for its unique splendor. Interior designer Jean Jongeward was designing an office for Bagley Wright, businessman and civic leader, who was then assembling one of the region's great private art collections.[16] Jean's design for his office was to have a floor of black walnut, in a pattern that was determined by furniture shapes and locations. All else would be bronze. Having worked with Ralph Anderson, she knew Gordon from his days in that office, and she had done interiors for three of his projects including his

first house for Jane and Pat Rogers. She asked for his assistance in detailing the unusual material in the Wright design, and asked, too, for the occasional critique. Wall surfaces were sheets of bronze; trim was bronze angles and flat bars, attached to a concealed armature by exposed aligned bronze screws. The lower edge of the bronze crown molding was a track with sliding clips, to hang a rotating selection of art from Wright's collection. The completed office was glorious, Jean's own favorite of all of her work.

Quite aside from individual projects, however, Gordon and Jim introduced into their professional practice a feature common to university design studios: they decided at the outset that Thursday afternoons would be dedicated to critiques of the office's projects. Comments were to be unreservedly candid, accepted as such without animosity or defensiveness, and each critiqued project would be presented again the following week, with challenged issues addressed. Jim and Gordon were serious about the idea; these were not to be "my, isn't that nice" afternoons. Inevitably these sessions grew into discussions touching on any project that posed issues of unusual interest. Sometimes friends and colleagues were invited; sometimes they just dropped by. In its earliest years the office was small—a receptionist and maybe a dozen architects—and Gordon thought the critiques worked best in those days, less well as the office grew. Through the critiques, and the quality of the executed projects themselves, Olson/Walker became known as an office of serious constructive inquiry, a place of good ideas, of sound, often

51

3.8 Albert Wickersham, the Maynard Building, Seattle, Washington, 1892; Olson/Walker, renovation, 1972–75. The building was named for Dr. David Swinson "Doc" Maynard—one of Seattle's earliest settlers and friend of Suquamish Chief Sealth, after whom Seattle was (more or less) named, at Maynard's urging. Photograph by Joshua Polansky.

inspired, work. To say that it became a model of creative architectural practice might overstate the case by a whisker, but the phrase comes to mind. Many young and talented architects who would later find their own way to outstanding reputations came to the office seeking a position; Olson/Walker could draw from a good talent pool. Gordon regarded everyone in the office as a colleague rather than an employee, and this was particularly true of Rick Sundberg and, at a later date, Bill Hook. Both would play important roles in the office's work.

The practice of weekly "crits" became a model for many offices in the city. Although few or none had the rigor of those at Olson/Walker, they fostered a citywide architectural environment both collaborative and competitive. (Gordon saw this as a half-conscious perpetuation of the habits of the prior generation's Puget Sound School.[17] But neither Gordon's own work, nor that of the partnership, reveal much outward evidence of that ancestry.)

Just months after Olson/Walker's inception Bill Sloan, one of Gordon's teachers from his university years at Idaho and still teaching there, was granted a sabbatical leave. To take his place in the design studio, he arranged to have Gordon invited as instructor for the 1970–71 academic year. Gordon moved his family to Moscow that September, and for nine months did the two jobs, teaching, and commuting to Seattle to fulfill his obligation to the new practice, an obligation made somewhat easier by his ability to derive a project's basic design unusually rapidly. Among Gordon's students at Idaho was Scott Fife, who turned to art rather than architecture, and later would do a sculpture that would play a small role in Gordon's life.

The third floor of the Maud Building was a floor of architects. To economize on payroll they shared an office manager, Marian Maestretti, who was also involved in a restaurant business. In 1969 she, Gwenyth Davis (later Gwenyth Bassetti), Marian Boyer, and Gordon, formed a partnership to create a restaurant, the Bakery. It was to be in the Richardsonian Romanesque Grand Central Building on First Avenue, one of Pioneer Square's finer buildings. Gordon designed the restaurant's interior to reflect its location, and in December of 1970 brought over architecture students from Idaho, on their Christmas break, to build the restaurant.

That may have been a consideration in the choice of Olson/Walker, and particularly Gordon, in 1972, for rehabilitation of the Maynard Building, the finest of Pioneer Square's early buildings (3.8, 3.9). Designed by Albert Wickersham in 1892, and superbly built, it is a more suave design, more up-to-date in its time, than the Richardsonian Romanesque Pioneer Building, its more famous neighbor. The Maynard commission was a large one for the office, in its physical size, in the complexities of its style—Richardson with a hint of Sullivan—and in its demand for studied design interventions. The building's seismic resistance needed to be brought up to current standards, as did mechanical and electrical systems, exiting, and elevators. These changes had to be done, but they could not be seen to have been done. Interior woodwork had to be refurbished, some of it replaced. The building's masonry, while sound and solid, needed much cosmetic attention, including water washing but not

3.9 The Maynard Building; fine and elaborate woodwork at the entry, a typical example of the contractor's skill and care in restoration. Photograph by Andrew van Leeuwen.

3.10 Olson/Walker, Gordon Walker, the Smith town houses, Seattle, 1975–76. Order, complexity, and visual poetry. Photograph by Andrew van Leeuwen.

sandblasting, which would have eroded the building's detailing. Supervision, at least, was not a concern: The general contractor, Fleming Sorensen, was one of the finest craftsmen to be found anywhere, and he gave his best efforts to the restoration of this exquisite building. Bob Wagoner, who would become known for his experience in restoration, was project architect. The project received a 1976 AIA National Honor Award, one of the institute's most prestigious, and the first of the many that would come to the Olson/Walker office.

Robert Smith owned a double lot on the west side of Seattle's Tenth Avenue. He and Gordon met at about the time of Olson/Walker's founding. By 1975 they were talking about Smith's property often and at length. Gordon prepared a scheme early on, in his mind and in sketches, but he thought nothing would come of it. He didn't think Smith was ready to build, until one day Smith was.

Tenth Avenue is an arterial that bisects an area of remarkable architectural quality in the region of Smith's site. The site lies well north of Capitol Hill's business district, and a block south of the buildings centered on Saint Mark's Cathedral. Some of those buildings, acquired by the diocese over time, are of no interest, but the cathedral itself, and the diocese offices, originally the rectory, are very special indeed—as an Elizabethan interpretation, the rectory has no equal in the Northwest. It has, as neighbors to the north, other organizational and educational buildings, some of them also of unusual quality. On the opposite side of Tenth Avenue, elegant walls of brick and stone shield from passersby some of Seattle's finest residential properties.

Smith's site was zoned for single-family dwellings. He wanted to develop it as residences, but as town houses, not detached units. He obtained relatively easily a rezoning that would allow as many as six units. He wanted to do just three. Gordon thought three would "look lonesome"—the property ought to offer its considerable amenities more widely. He had already decided four units would be ideal, and had thought through, and drawn, a promising unit plan and a resultant site plan. Gordon showed Smith his drawings, and described his reasoning. He brought Smith into agreement.

In most major cities including Seattle, multiunit housing projects have long been subject to a policy that the façade and its cornice be broken into a number of elements to suggest a group of smaller buildings. Thus any town house group Gordon might design for Smith could not present to the street a single planar façade. Gordon had no such façade in mind. What he had in mind was Wright's Unity Temple; he thought its composition of relatively complex forms, reprised at a smaller scale, might satisfy the policy, and nicely echo Saint Mark's.

He also had in mind a similar material: Unity Temple is poured-in-place concrete; Gordon wanted to build the town houses of concrete block. Smith did not; he felt it would be utterly out of place in the genteel setting. They found agreement on a design with few of Gordon's preconceptions. It would be of conventional wood-frame construction, and would look nothing like Unity Temple. It was driven by the site's contours. The site drops steeply at the rear, but the cornice of the steep slope is farther from the sidewalk at the southern edge of the lot than at the north. Gordon realized that since the setback of the southernmost unit could be greater than the northernmost, one could create a sequence of four intimately scaled identical façades stepping forward from south to north. The order established by this stepped sequence, and the complexities of the façades, are the keys to the project's success (3.10, 3.11). Each unit is entered from a private micro-courtyard, accessed under a wisteria-smothered arbor that visually links the units. Within the courtyard, fin walls, and a double height panel containing the entry door, shift one's perception to the vertical (3.12). Gordon's wish for concrete was satisfied, somewhat, by facing the units with stucco, faux-concrete. Unity Temple aside, there is a good bit of Wright in this project, in the dominant horizontals of the cantilevered roofs and pergolas, punctuated by the entry verticals, and the consequent feeling of peace and privacy, even on a busy thoroughfare.

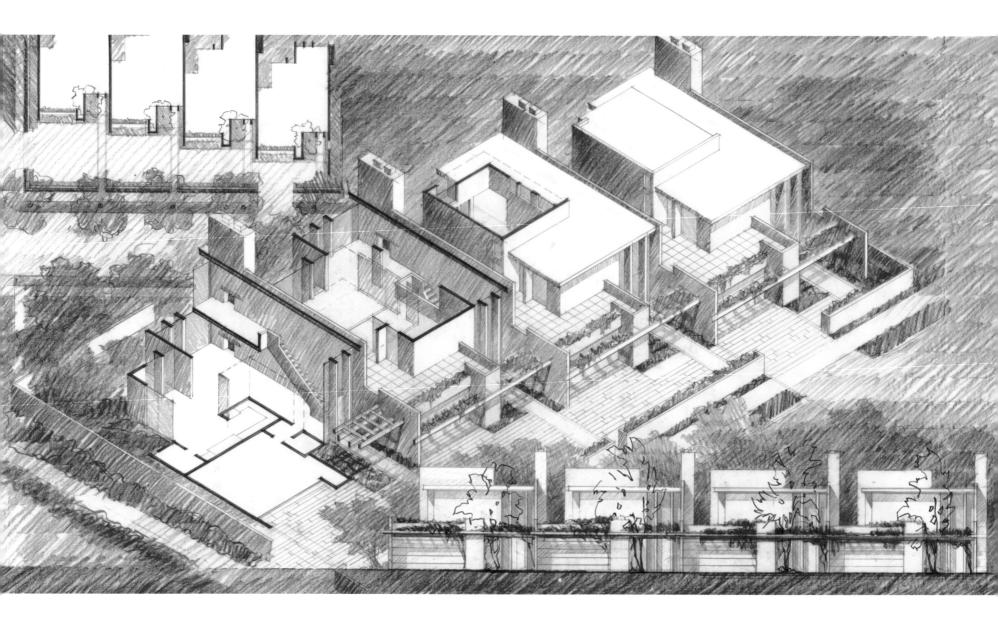

3.11 The Smith town houses, diagrammatic drawing by Bill Hook.

3.12 The Smith town houses; an entry. The low beams establish an intimacy on approach, and a space of privacy beyond. Photograph by Andrew van Leeuwen.

In 1975 Olson/Walker became involved in the rehabilitation of Seattle's Good Shepherd Center and its considerable campus. Built in 1906 as the Home of the Good Shepherd, it had provided shelter and support to young women in need of either, until it closed in 1973. The city purchased the property through the formation of the Historic Seattle Preservation and Development Authority. In planning the rehabilitation Gordon worked with colleague Bob Wagoner, who had participated in the Maynard project. Because the Pacific Northwest Ballet was a tenant in the building, Gordon became a friend of its founders, Kent Stowell and Francia Russell. He would also establish a relationship with the city that would lead to other projects, among them the rehabilitation of an exhibition hall at the Seattle Center for Stowell and Russell's PNB.

Gordon and Jim had wanted to do a significant project in the city, and with the help of Jim's father, who held the deed, they had a site available for development at the north edge of Seattle's Pike Place Market. Katherine Olson managed the empty land as a parking lot. The original idea was to do an office building with a bakery at ground level, probably in part because of Gordon's experience in designing the Bakery restaurant. But because the market needed residential stock, Victor Steinbrueck recommended changing the use to residential and retail, thereby smoothing the project's acceptance by the Pike Place Market Preservation and Development Authority. Gale

3.13 Olson/Walker, the Pike and Virginia Building, Seattle, 1974–75, from the north side of Virginia Street. Jim's unit was at the top of the taller element. Gordon's unit, above the plant-laden marquee, was originally entered from the Virginia Street sidewalk at the juncture of the low and high elements. Photograph by Andrew van Leeuwen.

3.14 The Pike and Virginia Building, the deck of Jim Olson's top-floor apartment, with a view of the east coast of Japan. Photograph by Dick Busher.

Cool helped with the sea of paperwork. (For a time they considered calling the office Cool Olson Walker. But the acronym—COW—was against it, and Gale decided not to join the partnership.)

This time there was no difference of opinion about materials: Jim and Gordon agreed that the building should be of concrete. Jim was intensely interested in creating a design that would seem integral to the market. He established the building's essential configuration: a lower volume on Pike Place would retain something of the existing cornice height along the street, and a higher eastern element would optimize revenues. Aesthetically, Jim and Gordon shared a belief that the building should have a sense of the vernacular; it should be spare, absent any ostentation or affectation. Gordon thought this would be much determined by the building's structure and construction, how the building would go together. Because of his experience with larger building design, Rick Sundberg was lured from the office of Ibsen Nelson:

They hired me for three months in June 1974, to work on Pike and Virginia. After three months, Jim Olson said, "Let's go have a beer," and invited me to stay. There were lots of iterations, and the project was put on the shelf until Jim could finance $990K for the shell. We hired the contractor—Eberharter[18]—they were the ones who suggested we do the pans [forms for concrete poured in place]. We were looking at other details—in precast [concrete]. But they suggested pans. Gordon wanted block, I wanted metal. We kind of made it up as we went along. Gordon and I had a few glasses of wine over that project. If you pull it apart, everything was based on the dimensions of the pans. Gordon's unit was the anomaly, with the glass [block] and canted wall. If you build a frame, you can do a lot with it. Gordon taught me to think about craft, and not to give up on it until it was correct. I would carry that ethic through my career. The lessons were really good. How to build this little building, tiny, really. I didn't see the beauty of the building at first; it took about five years. That building gave me lessons in

architecture. I like that little building. We were just young guys, in our 30s. We were just three kids.

We got an honor award! We weren't expecting it.

I saw the Raff house before I met Gordon. I wondered how he talked them into it.[19]

The building would be out of place anywhere else (3.13). It is a part of the market, and as a part of the market it is a perfect building: timeless, impossible to date, blending seamlessly with its companions. It received an AIA Seattle Honor award in 1979.

On the building's completion twelve units were sold as unfinished shells. Gordon and Jim each retained a unit. Jim chose the penthouse for his home, finishing it in elegance, its glass claiming spectacular views across Elliott Bay to Bainbridge Island and the distant Olympic Range (3.14). Gordon's choice was just above the ground-floor retail spaces on Pike Place, although the unit is entered directly from the Virginia Street sidewalk. There is a view of very short reach, into the market's vitality (3.15), and a long view westward across Elliott Bay (3.16).

In working through the design, Gordon was thinking of Pierre Chareau's House of Glass, La Maison de Verre, of 1930–32, in Paris, whose extensive walls of glass and glass-block-like units give it its entirely appropriate name. Gordon hadn't seen the building itself, although he did get as close as the gate, but the building was published with very complete photographs. Accepting the Pike and Virginia Building's absolute boundaries of poured-in-place concrete, and defining by storefront glazing systems and walls of glass block, Gordon created spaces both robust and delicate, dense and luminous. The glass block provided privacy—minimal—while allowing light to reach the rear of the unit, where another wall of glass block was artificially backlit. Believing that much of daily life takes place at one table or another, Gordon designed a long wooden one that linked the kitchen and living area; its vastly oversized concrete piers hold their own against the building's structure. The table was

of locally milled alder, as were other furnishings, casework, and flooring. A patio was carved out along the south party wall. Its double height drew in additional light;[20] more importantly it was a space that invited contemplation — of the character imparted by glass block, of the structural order of the building, of the life of the market, of Gordon's cooking.

By the mid-1970s Gordon's professional life was thriving. He was a founding partner in an admired firm, he had recognition, awards — he could justly believe he had influenced the architectural quality of the region. His personal life was not doing equally well. Bobbie was in part Native American, and had become involved in the history and rituals of her ancestry. In Gordon's absorbed dedication to his work he had not set aside time to understand or support her interests. Their paths had diverged. They divorced in 1978.

3.15 The Pike and Virginia Building, Gordon Walker's apartment: concrete, glass block, and a very big table. The windows at right look out to a terrace above Pike Place and the market. Photograph by Gordon Walker.

3.16 Gordon's apartment; the view westward across Elliott Bay to West Seattle and, on a clear day, the Olympic Range. Photograph by Gordon Walker.

4 OLSON/WALKER 1978–85

OLSON/WALKER DESIGNED MYRIAD PROJECTS from 1978 to 1985. Six are essential to this story.

The Aqua Theater at the south end of Seattle's Green Lake, built in 1950 to a design by George Stoddard, comprised a semi-circular concrete grandstand seating 5,200, and two four-story diving platforms. It had been built quickly to be available for the first Seafair celebration that summer. Over the years it was used for jazz festivals, outdoor plays, musicals, July Fourth celebrations, but attendance diminished with the passing years, maintenance became occasional, and in 1969 the grandstand was declared unsafe. The site pleaded for some kind of renovation that would exploit its rich potential. Because of its unique intrinsic interest, Gordon had twice framed it as a problem for design studios he taught on occasion at the university.

In 1978 Olson/Walker were selected, from a number of competing firms, to make the site a sailing and boating facility, abandoning any theatrical purpose. It was to be Gordon's project. His design called for demolition of three-fourths of the grandstand, the remainder to be left as a ruin, with new buildings, appropriately utilitarian in materials and form, to be built on the theater's foundations. Exposed trusses above the flat roofs of the single-story buildings minimize the visual intrusion of the new work, preserving views of the lake. The trusses radiate to rest on a concrete colonnade that frames a bit of the lake's walking path, tying the structure to the circumnavigation of the lake. Spaces between buildings access the docks, for visitors, rowers, boaters, and fisherpersons.

The remaining portion of the grandstand provides casual seating for contemplation, conversation, and lunch-eating. One truncated structural rib is left intact, with a single row of steps for climbing. At the top is artist Bob Jensen's giant oar, called *Stroke*, counterbalanced, pivoting on its base in the wind. The compelling kinetic sculpture, and the experience of climbing around the ruin, satisfy the adventurous (4.1, 4.2).

In 1980 Olson/Walker submitted the facility for an AIA award. Philip Johnson was the sole juror. Slides and drawings were submitted to Johnson's New York office in the Seagram Building. A video of his process shows him shuffling through the submissions quickly, discarding many without a second glance: "I don't do branch banks." Acknowledging the Green Lake project's success, Johnson is shown awarding it a Citation, while mumbling about "architecture by destruction."[21]

In 1979 Robin Woodward, another of Gordon's good friends, asked him to become a partner in a venture with her and Illsley Nordstrom; they were to open a wine bar, Seattle's first, in a space on Fourth Avenue leased from Paul Schell. Gordon would provide a design, help to organize construction, and do some of it. The space was narrow—the width of a single store-front—deep front-to-back, and two stories in height, with concrete half-columns with pronounced capitals[22] ranged along both sides—not promising as

a configuration for a wine bar. In trying to make it one, the obvious strategy would be to dedicate one side of the space to circulation, the other to the bar itself, with the familiar display of bottles ranged against the wall. But Gordon was not interested in dealing with the challenge "by cramming everything up to one side. I really wanted to deal with it right down the zipper." Along the centerline of the space, Gordon built the two-sided bar, an illuminated prism of glass block framed in green-painted steel, its geometry rectangular, with 45-degree corners and transitions to the wider center (4.3, 4.4). Wine displays are awkward with the scheme, and with a crowd there is inevitable jostling in the circulation paths along the edges, but the seating is roughly double what it would be in a conventional arrangement. Beyond the bar a flight of stairs, also built by Gordon, leads to a small dining space, defined by half-columns at the corners (4.5). Above, Gordon floods the column capitals with light, drawing the eye to the open upper reaches, emphasizing

4.1 Olson/Walker, Gordon Walker, the Green Lake Sailing and Boating Facility, Seattle, 1978–79. Photograph by Andrew van Leeuwen.

4.2 Green Lake Sailing and Boating Facility, Jensen's "Stroke" rises at left. The Green Lake walking path continues at right. Photograph by Andrew van Leeuwen.

4.3 Olson/Walker, Gordon Walker, The 1904 Restaurant, Seattle, Washington, 1979 (much altered). Photograph by Dick Busher.

4.4 The 1904, looking down from the small dining room. Photograph by Dick Busher.

4.5 The 1904; The upper-floor dining room, and the stair that leads to it, can be seen more easily here. Photograph by Dick Busher.

the height of the space, and the capitals' elegant geometry. The lower zone is complexity, activity, varied murmurs, crowded movement, now and again a voice raised, much clinking of glasses. Above, all is tranquility.

Paul Schell, owner of the 1904 site, had been the attorney for The Bakery project. He and Gordon had become friends. With the Pike and Virginia and 1904 projects completed, Gordon discussed doing more architectural work with Paul. Paul and his partner, Jim Youngren, responded far beyond Gordon's expectations, flooding the Olson/Walker office with commissions for projects in Seattle, Tacoma, and Portland. One of these arose from a 1979 City of Seattle request for proposals for a project in the Pike Place Market area that would include residential and commercial spaces and parking for 200 vehicles. Olson/Walker's proposal, developed in

partnership with Schell's Cornerstone Development Company and Ball Landau Young Construction, won the commission. Gordon and Rick Sundberg would lead the design team.

The 27,000-square-foot site (4.6) fronts on Western Avenue's west side, immediately below the market and just south of the Pike and Virginia Building. The land falls away in a forty-five-foot drop to the west, toward the waterfront and Elliott Bay. The

4.6 Olson/Walker, Gordon Walker, and Cornerstone Development Company, Hillclimb Court, Seattle, Washington, 1980–82: as seen from the market. Photograph by Andrew van Leeuwen.

OLSON/WALKER 1978–85

west side of the site presents another and greater problem: it abuts the elevated, heavily trafficked Alaskan Way Viaduct that runs along the waterfront, so traffic noise is severe. Views to Elliott Bay would be possible only from floors well above the Western Avenue elevation, and then at the cost of some noise. Rick Sundberg thought it was "the world's crummiest site to put a building on." The pedestrian "Hillclimb" from the waterfront to the market is on the site's north border, hence the project's name: Hillclimb Court. The character of the design reprises the Pike and Virginia Building, with the slightest nod to The 1904: an exposed modular poured-in-place concrete frame is neighbored with steel, glass, glass block, and commercial storefront systems (4.7, 4.8). Gordon noted: "The materials, the structure of the building, are all about context and urbanism. The notion was that it should be visually supportive of the concrete frames of its neighbors." The exterior materials, the concrete especially, do a reasonable job of abating

4.7 Hillclimb Court: looking east; the entry from the sidewalk is at lower left. Photograph by Andrew van Leeuwen.

the viaduct's roar. But the real key to the building's livability—more than that, its delight—is the courtyard (4.8–4.10). All thirty-five units face a courtyard whose verdure and fountain recall the "urban fabric" that had thrilled Gordon in his long-ago first trip to Europe. The courtyard's dimensions are generous enough to make it useful, children can genuinely play in it, while the fountain, and the planters with their green and growing things, give it intimacy. And it is an egalitarian courtyard. The units vary in size, from about 550 to about 1,150 square feet, but the courtyard's palette of materials continues into all alike, giving the sense that it is an outdoor extension of each. There is no misstep in this design.

69

4.8 Hillclimb Court: the courtyard, looking south. Photograph by
Andrew van Leeuwen.

4.9 Hillclimb Court: the unit façades.
Photograph by Andrew van Leeuwen.

4.10 Hillclimb Court: looking southwest. Photograph by Andrew van
Leeuwen.

Gordon married again, to Terri Siegl, in 1980, while Hillclimb Court was being built. She was the original receptionist for Olson/ Walker, a brilliant woman and a very busy one: Leaving Olson/ Walker in 1978, she taught secondary school Greek and Latin while working toward an M.Arch. at the university. Son Ian was born to them in 1982. In 1984 they moved into Hillclimb Court's two-story unit 103, directly off the courtyard, "building it out" as a home for themselves. Ian rode his tricycle around the fountain.

Hillclimb Court received an AIA Seattle Honor Award in 1983; the following year it was published in *Architectural Record*, and was featured in the Japanese *GA* [Global Architecture] Houses volume for that year, a considerable honor. Its entry, and its extensively treated courtyard—elements of the design that did not produce revenue directly—meant that in comparison with a typical apartment or condominium development, Hillclimb was expensive. Paul Schell thought it was overly so. On its completion he told Gordon that Cornerstone could not do any more "award-winning architecture." Yet in the longer view the project's appeal has meant an appropriate return on its cost. Almost without exception, owners of the units have given the building first-rate maintenance over the years and decades, and have been grateful for the time they have lived there. Only rarely and briefly does a unit appear on the market.

When Olson/Walker won the Hillclimb Court competition, they moved the office to the Fix-Madore building, a prior

4.11 Olson/Walker and NBBJ, Merrill Place, 1984. The north building, at right, is the Schwabacher Hardware Company of 1905, by Bebb and Mendel. Photograph by Andrew van Leeuwen.

4.12 Merrill Place, Bebb's Sullivan-esque Schwabacher entry. Photograph by Andrew van Leeuwen.

development project of the Cornerstone Group, on Western Avenue across from the Hillclimb Court site and the Hillclimb walk. The building was ideally located for managing the Hillclimb project, and Gordon further thought the owner would benefit from their support. The new office was on the second floor of the Madore side of the building (the Fix side is residential condominiums; the merged buildings share an elevator and other support spaces). The building is beautiful in its way, a spare concrete shell with large industrial steel sash windows. Gordon recalled that in designing the space for their use, the idea was to respect the shell of the building, imagining the new office as a composition of objects floating within the old concrete framework, the furniture easily dismantled and moved. Olson/Walker's previously informal,

4.13 HOWDI, the Olympic Block, Seattle, 1985–87. The building at right, now known as the Yesler Building, was originally the Bank of Commerce. Its lower two floors, from 1890–91, are by Elmer Fisher. The third floor, added in 1906, is by Albert Wickersham, architect of the Maynard Building. Photograph by Andrew van Leeuwen.

completely open office was perfect for individual clients, and although the firm had grown and was dealing with clients accustomed to a more traditional office setting, the space remained open. The office would grow to occupy the first floor as well, fronting on Alaskan Way and the waterfront.

Olson/Walker had designed the Pike and Virginia Building and Hillclimb Court to the satisfaction of the Pike Place Market Authority, and had brought back to splendid life the Maynard Building in Pioneer Square. In 1984 they collaborated with NBBJ on renovation of the Schwabacher Hardware Company's warehouse, two blocks south of the Maynard Building (4.11). The development would be known as Merrill Place. Its adaptation to retail, commercial, and residential uses would help to anchor the southern part of the district. The building's entry, at the right edge of the First Avenue façade, is a handsome exercise in the Sullivanesque. Charles H. Bebb of Bebb and Mendel, the original architects, had come to Seattle in 1893 from Louis Sullivan's office in Chicago (4.12)[23] to represent Sullivan's Opera House design. When the project failed, Bebb stayed on, eventually to cofound Bebb and Gould.

The center of the Pioneer Square district has always been understood to be the small triangular park on First Avenue at Yesler Street. Its east face is created by the Pioneer Building, west is the Mutual Life Building. On a Sunday morning in 1972, the turn-of-the-century Olympic Block, which was the southern face of the triangular park, quietly collapsed. The site, only partly cleared

of debris, stood empty for years thereafter, surrounded by an unhandsome plywood fence. In 1985 Jim and Gordon joined then owners and architects David Hewitt, Jim Daly, and Bill Isley to embark on the design of a replacement for the fence and debris. They adopted the acronym HOWDI. The project turned out to be a complicated one. The program would include the two contiguous buildings to the south, and would comprise mostly office and retail space, with some high-end condominiums (4.13).

But since the location is what it is, the design was under much pressure, many faces looked over many shoulders. HOWDI developed a particularly happy six-story design, whose top floors were set back behind brick screens, the intervening spaces becoming decks. But with the consequent loss of revenue-producing square footage, the design failed to pencil out, and it lacked any evident reference to the context. It was set aside. The cast of characters grew, as Victor Steinbrueck and Folke Nyberg became involved. There were more and deeper disagreements, lengthily debated, compromises only slowly worked out; there were delays, a lot of them. The Olson/Walker office had grown to thirty-five, payroll and overhead continued as always, there was very little billable work, income was nil. Money must be found. Gordon had nothing like the resources needed to make a contribution proportional to his position. Feeling great personal stress, he resigned from the firm. Jim Olson invited Rick Sundberg to replace Gordon, and Olson/Walker became Olson Sundberg.

5 GORDON 1985—90

IN 1985, OLSON/WALKER HAVING BECOME OLSON/SUNDBERG, and with nothing on Gordon's drawing board, he, Terri, and three-year-old Ian went off to Italy. They could afford it—they needed little more than airfare—because of the University of Washington's interests there. Architect Astra Zarina, graduate of the university, had become one of its most inspiring faculty and one of the profession's most talented designers.[24] She created the Rome Studies Program for the Department of Architecture in 1970, and had been its director since, dividing her time between Rome, Seattle, and a spacious villa complex in Civita di Bagnoregio, one of Italy's most romantic hill towns. Civita is also one of the smallest and the most isolated, accessed only by a pedestrian bridge across a daunting chasm (5.1). When Astra first became interested in the town, it had long been in decline, and it was losing area, as bits of its edges were slipping away to the plain below. Astra devoted her considerable abilities to the revival of the town, finding means to stabilize the land to some degree, and restoring many of the town's properties. One of them was a stone house, centuries old, clinging to the edge of the mesa near the footbridge. The owner was Gunnar Birkerts, fellow Latvian American, a renowned architect in his own right, who so respected Astra's abilities that he asked her to design the striking renovation of the house. There Gordon, Terri, and Ian drifted through three princely months. They spent many evenings in Astra's villa among the small, spontaneous groups, townspeople and students that gathered there. Gordon remembers doing a lot of the cooking for those candlelit evenings, but never all of it. Astra's cooking was of a piece with her other talents—students in the Rome Program had to learn to prepare at least one local recipe—and her artichoke lasagna and Monte Bianco were glories not soon forgotten.

Back in Seattle's real world, Gordon rented a space in Hillclimb Court as an office, and began seeking work. He consulted on some Olson/Walker projects, including the university's Applied Physics Laboratory, and was one of three finalists in a competition for Mercer Island's City Hall.[25] Then, in 1985, Pat James, NBBJ's

design lead, who had worked with Gordon on Merrill Place, invited him to join NBBJ's Seattle office.

Projects at Olson/Walker had become successively larger and more complex over the years, but for decades NBBJ had been doing hospitals, schools, and forty-story office buildings. For Gordon the position would mean an entirely new project scale. It would also mean a very different corporate culture, for NBBJ was more exactly structured, less casual than Olson/Walker, as befit the management of larger projects within the larger office. Gordon was unsure about the offer; he sought advice from friends Peter Miller, Doug Raff, and Paul Schell. They said, at some length and in consensus, that this was a good chance to broaden his experience, that he should seize the offer, that this was an opportunity to learn more about "the business and marketing side of architecture." Gordon knew they were telling him he needed that, and he knew they were right. He followed the advice. So, a month and a half after returning

5.1 Bagnoregio, in the foreground, accesses the footbridge that leads to Civita on the horizon. The Birkerts house grasps the edge of the mesa just left of the bridge's point of arrival. Astra Zarina was architect for renovations in much of the town, including Birkerts' house, and her own extensive dwelling at the far end of Civita's only street. Photograph by Norman Johnston.

from Italy, Gordon closed the Hillclimb Court office. He would now be a "design principal," with a regular paycheck, a retirement plan, a support staff, and a car—all welcome curiosities for Gordon. Acknowledging, at last, the architectural establishment, he joined the AIA, though only briefly.

NBBJ had been founded in 1943 as Naramore, Bain, Brady, & Johanson. Floyd Naramore had been the architect of Seattle's

5.2 Paul Hayden Kirk, service building, Seattle Center, Washington, ca. 1961; Gordon Walker, headquarters, and practice and performance facility for the Pacific Northwest Ballet, 1987. Drawing by Bill Hook.

public schools in an era of unprecedented school building from 1919 to 1934. When Gordon joined the firm, NBBJ were still doing schools, including projects for higher education. They were also doing large-scale corporate and commercial work, and civic work and planning, and were acquiring what would be an ongoing national reputation for expertise in hospital design. They had become one of the largest firms in the United States, with offices in seven cities. Gordon thought of this experience as his "finishing school" in architectural practice. The Seattle office had a "Design Group," something between a think tank and a research and development component, that was given time and resources to travel, and to research and discuss design theory. The group adopted from Olson/Walker the practice of weekly critiques, though in this case their sessions were better described as scheduled and structured discussions. As a design principal, Gordon was invited to join the group. He said, in one of the gatherings, that architecture was, for him, a little like making meatloaf—add a little of this, a little of that, until the balance was right. He added, candidly but undiplomatically, that architecture at NBBJ seemed like adding oregano at the end of the process. The group became known as "Oregano."

Gordon had a previous commission to complete before he could commit his full time to NBBJ. Kent Stowell and Francia Russell had founded the Pacific Northwest Ballet in the mid 1970s. Gordon met them at that time, during the rehabilitation of the Good Shepherd Center, where they had their offices. He

has been involved in the PNB's facilities ever since. "We are still friends…I hope." He was designing what Kent and Francia called the ballet's headquarters at the Seattle Center; Brent Rogers was assisting with the project. It was to be a renovation of a space within one of the workaday buildings at the center, a building designed by Paul Hayden Kirk, whose work Gordon had admired since his college days. But the Seattle Center building is not typical of Kirk's work. His legend is based on his uniquely elegant architecture of wood; the Center building's dominant feature is the folded plate roof of reinforced concrete, a structural cliché from the 1950s. Kirk gave the idea a fresh life by introducing narrow flat areas between the diagonal panels (5.2). Steel reinforcing at the tops and bottoms of the diagonals is what makes the geometry function as a beam, and this is felt intuitively, from everyday experiences with folded paper. Kirk's atypical flat areas at top and bottom give expression to this intuitive understanding—and provide a roomy housing for the steel reinforcing bars. Gordon accepted the underside of Kirk's structure as the ceiling of the ballet's administration office, seven practice rooms, and a performance hall.

The first project NBBJ put in Gordon's hands was a formidable one. The office had been hired to design a pair of towers on a full city block in downtown Seattle. The client was the landholding division of the Canadian Pacific Railway. This experience entailed several firsts for Gordon: he was working in a large corporate design firm; he was working on a high-profile project for an international

5.3 NBBJ, Marathon Towers, Seattle, 1985–87 (not built). Drawing by Bill Hook.

5.4 Marathon Towers. Drawing by Bill Hook.

client—and he was working under NBBJ partner Bill Bain—William Bain Jr.—son of founding partner William Bain Sr. Gordon bought an anti-intimidation three-piece suit, deep blue, with pinstripes. The Marathon Towers proceeded well through design development (5.3, 5.4), but a slow economy and an oversupply of office space in downtown Seattle put the project on the shelf. The site would be occupied, eventually, by the Benaroya concert hall designed by LMN Architects of Seattle. The Marathon design would have a slight degree of influence on later NBBJ tower projects, including Two Union Square of 1987 in Seattle, also designed under Bill Bain's direction.

Of NBBJ's seven branch offices, the one in Palo Alto was headed by partner John Pangrazio, who focused the office on medical buildings. He had secured and was managing the commission for Stanford University's Medical Center, then nearing completion. Gordon was brought in with the expectation that he would find new work; both he and John wanted to extend the office's range. Gordon thought the office should move from Palo Alto to downtown San Francisco, as a location more central to developing projects. He found a space in the Halladie Building (5.5). Designed in 1917 by Willis Polk, the building was the first in America to use curtain wall construction. But Polk equally had an eye for elegance—the

MARATHON CROWN CENTER

5.5 Willis Polk, the Halladie Building, San Francisco, 1917; rehabilitation 2014. Photograph by Gabriel Moulin, taken shortly after the building's completion.

And having moved into the Halladie Building and having a role with NBBJ, Gordon was asked by Kathie and Doug Raff to do a second house for them, this one on Whidbey Island. Gordon's Whidbey design (assisted by T. William Booth) is one story of conventional frame construction, far removed from the three-story concrete-block house built in Seattle thirteen years earlier; the two houses seem to have nothing in common. Yet they do, at a deeply fundamental level, because the Whidbey house is also a highly ordered yet very complex composition. The waterfront façade reveals an order whose permutations permeate the design (5.7). An overriding ABCBA rhythm is established by paired shed roofs. A second DEDEDED rhythm is created by the paired piers of the porch. The paired shed roofs correlate with the first and third E bays of the porch but not its middle E bay. The two rhythmic orders are integrated, softened, and enriched by the trellis, continuous but projecting at the D bays, that owes much to the Smith town houses. And there is a still more complexly ordered reading. If we consider the paired shed roofs as three elements rather than one, the rhythm is an asymmetrical ABCDABCDA. Yet because B is the reverse of D, the composition itself is symmetrical about the centerline of the middle A (5.8, 5.9, 5.10).

In 1986 the office was commissioned to design a building, L-shaped in plan, that would complete a square in downtown Palo Alto. The city was architecturally conservative: zoning laws mandated a Spanish Revival character in the area encompassing the project. Gordon completed a design that was as much his own as would pass the review board—and to this he added, in the resulting open square, a "folly": a small flower shop. He liked it, and the idea became a habit. Many of Gordon's subsequent large-scale projects would include a similar "folly," to bring an element of intimacy to buildings accommodating large numbers of occupants.

And there was a more personal folly. Gordon's longtime friend Peter Miller and longtime office compatriot Colleen Madden were married in July 1987, on Paul Schell's property adjacent

Halladie is a beautiful design. The space Gordon had found was small, therefore crowded, but he remembers it as "exquisite." Over time he and John began to instill a more casual culture into the office. The partners in Seattle were not of the same school of thought; Gordon and John were reminded that the office must represent NBBJ's corporate image.

to Peter's own home near Langley on Whidbey Island. Gordon designed and, with the assistance of Brent Rogers, built a lovely shingled gazebo to enshrine the couple for the occasion. The little structure lies across a narrow escarpment, so the floor that is at grade on the higher land (5.10) is at a commanding elevation on the other (5.11).

In their quest to broaden the range of the San Francisco office, John and Gordon began responding to requests for proposals from colleges and universities. After several failed attempts, they found success: they made the short list, then were awarded the commission, for a research building at the University of California's Davis Medical Center in Sacramento. Although site master planning was not part of the contract, Gordon typically considered the larger context in designing the building, and he argued that that should be the case here. His argument was convincing; the project would include both the research building and a provisional master

5.6 Gordon Walker, house II for Katherine and Douglass Raff, Whidbey Island, Puget Sound, 1979, waterfront façade; rhythmic orders and complexities. Photograph by Andrew van Leeuwen.

5.7 Raff house II; a bedroom, a typical half-gable interior. The angled brace locks the structure against lateral forces. Photograph by Andrew van Leeuwen.

5.8 Raff house II, dining space, complex symmetry. Photograph by Andrew van Leeuwen.

5.9 Raff house II, living space, complex symmetry. Photograph by Andrew van Leeuwen.

5.10 Gordon Walker, the gazebo for Colleen and Peter's wedding, Langley, Whidbey Island, Puget Sound, 1987. Photograph by Andrew van Leeuwen.

5.11 The Langley gazebo. Photograph by Andrew van Leeuwen.

plan. That, in turn, must have impressed: NBBJ were commissioned to design a second research building, and to prepare a visualization of an entire academic campus (5.12). For Gordon and the office, this was the beginning of an extensive series of projects for the University of California—for UC Davis (5.13, 5.14), San Diego, and Riverside, with NBBJ, and the Irvine campus on his own.

The first of these came in 1988: The office was commissioned to design a new classroom and student services building for UC San Diego (5.15, 5.16). It was to be located at the entry end of a new "library walk" that would terminate at the library and student union building. Facing the walk, the building would offer a full range of student services, and would provide access for several thousand students per hour, coming and going from twenty-two classrooms. Gordon recalled fondly a design review from San Diego architect Rob Quigley, who noted that the design and coloration "looked like it came from a cool weather architect." The comment was banter between friends, but Gordon took it to heart. He decided he

should use accurate sun angles, rather than assumed conventions, for shades and shadows, to better determine depths of openings, and should consider at greater length the colors of the watercolor rendering. Gordon's work on the project continued through the design development phase.

But he was increasingly aware with each day's work that he chafed at the culture of the large office and was uncomfortable with the regimen. He wanted to design as the ideas came, work as early, or as late, as was necessary to complete an exploration. His difference with large-office practice was fundamental. In 1990 he decided to leave NBBJ, dropping, at the same time, his AIA membership. And there was another separation at that time, this one neither initiated by Gordon, nor wanted by him. "Terri was just tired of me. I had become overbearing and boring, a bad combination. She left, and we divorced."

When he had begun with NBBJ, Gordon's prowess as a hands-on "designer-builder," with a focus on materiality and craft, was legendary, a matter of record. His time with NBBJ added to that prowess a degree of experience in large-scale planning and large-scale buildings. It also gave Gordon a foundation on which to build a relationship with his alma mater, the University of Idaho. He began work on a Long-Range Campus Development Plan for Idaho while still in San Francisco, in coordination with landscape architects RHAA—Royston, Hanamoto, Alley, and Abey—in Mill Valley. This association would continue as the Idaho work evolved.

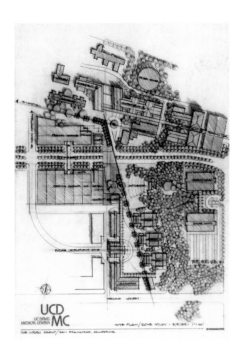

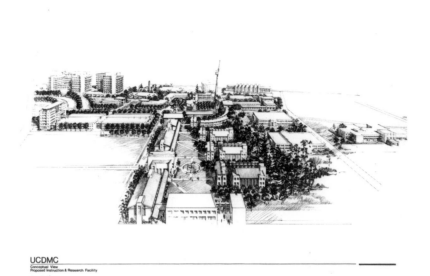

5.12 NBBJ, University of California Davis Medical Center master plan with research buildings, Sacramento, 1986. The bent line of trees defines and coheres both buildings and open spaces. Drawing by Gordon Walker.

5.13 UC Davis Medical Center, aerial view from the south. The drawing illustrates the strength of the diagonal line of repetitive buildings, and the tree line, which links them with the otherwise unrelated campus to the north, creating a geometrically ordered open space. Drawing by Bill Hook.

5.14 UC Davis Medical Center; a study of the typical exterior wall. Drawing by Bill Hook.

5.15 Color study, Classroom and Student Services Building, UC San Diego, California, watercolor by Bonnie Bridges, NBBJ.

5.16 Classroom and Student Services Building, UC San Diego. Photograph by NBBJ.

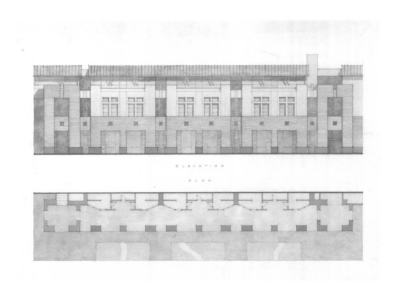

6 WALKER ARCHITECTURE

LEAVING NBBJ IN 1990 TO BEGIN INDEPENDENT PRACTICE for the first time since his preregistration days, Gordon set up an office on Sutter Street in San Francisco. In the mid-1980s he had met renowned Australian architect Glenn Murcutt, future Pritzker Prize recipient, and was impressed by Murcutt's purely one-man office: Murcutt designed, wrote specifications, supervised on sites, made coffee, answered the phone, wrote checks, and ran the copy machine. Gordon had learned much from NBBJ about how to manage and grow a practice, and this knowledge might have made a Murcutt-like office entirely possible. But Gordon's heart was in design, he chafed at time away from the board, so by his own admission he neglected other aspects of the practice. He would have been forced to give most of his time to design anyway, because he had a plethora of work: his design ability and his personality had brought projects to his drawing board. There was a residential remodeling in Seattle and two in California, a master plan for the Princeton Bio Center in Princeton, NJ, and a consulting role with the Castilleja School in Palo Alto.[26] In addition to that work, Gordon's reputation with key people at the University of California led to a commission, in association with Cannon Architects of Los Angeles, for a student recreation center on the Irvine campus. The student center further cemented his reputation with the university, and the one commission at Irvine led to two more. Son Colin had earned a five-year professional degree in architecture from the California College of the Arts in San Francisco in 1988, and although he was not registered, he had acquired some useful architectural experience. He joined his father in late 1990. They practiced as Walker Architecture.[27]

In 1991, still in San Francisco, Gordon submitted an article to Peter Staten and David Brewster for the *Seattle Weekly*. Paul Thiry, chief architect for the Century 21 Exposition of 1962, had not liked Gordon's adaptation of Kirk's exposition hall for use by the Pacific Northwest Ballet. Thiry would have been more upset by the *Weekly* article.[28] To him its futuristic theme would be best

6.1 Gordon Walker and RHAA, Campus Plan for the University of Idaho, Moscow, 1990–97. Olmsted's boulevard, Gordon's grand allée, is the diagonal at far right. Albertson Hall is below center, above the right end of the large cluster of trees, within the void of the U-shaped building. Drawing by Gordon Walker.

6.2 Detail of east park of the Idaho plan. Drawing by Gordon Walker.

served by making the grounds an ambience apart from the streets of Seattle; accordingly the Seattle Center has been closed off from its neighborhood since its inception. Gordon has long thought the center would benefit from a better integration with the city. Memorial Stadium is one of the closing elements, a seldom used structure that presents only a blind wall to the street. Gordon has proposed that it be removed, to open the former fairgrounds space to the sidewalk and the street. He suggests that a part of that space be taken for a concert hall and museum, or a similar building with daily use. With additional housing on the perimeter the center would be active, and would be seen to be active, at all times. This would also have the tremendous advantage that a view could be created to Elliott Bay and Bainbridge Island. The proposal is compelling. The Center has never realized its potential; Gordon's proposal would go a long way toward helping it to do so.

In long-ago 1904 Seattle had accepted from the Olmsted Brothers of Brookline, Massachusetts, a master plan for the city. The Olmsted Plan proposed an almost twenty-mile necklace of streets and boulevards linking the Lake Washington waterfront, five existing parks, thirty-two new ones including an arboretum, and the university's campus.[29] Of plans by the Olmsted Brothers, Seattle's is second only to Boston's in extent, condition, and importance to the city. Supported by an ongoing series of bond issues, the Seattle plan was carried through to near-completion by the late 1920s, and has been respected since. It remains by far the most important man-made element of the city's visual quality. John Charles Olmsted came to Seattle in 1903 to present the plan, and returned often thereafter to supervise construction of its elements until his death in 1920. In his western trip of 1908 he spent time in Moscow, Idaho, to design the university's first comprehensive campus plan, a project led by campus planning director Joanne Reece. Olmsted's Idaho plan addressed the center of the campus, and projected from it a boulevard, straight as a Roman road, extending southeast to the main road into Moscow proper.

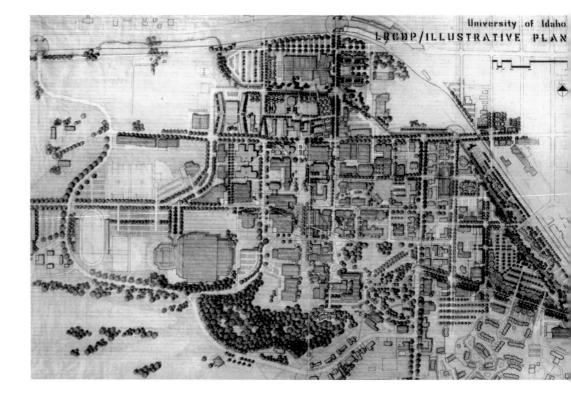

With the passage of the Great War, the Great Depression, World War II, the G.I. Bill, and Postmodernism, by 1990 Olmsted's plan had inevitably become compromised. Gordon said, "The entry to the historic center of the campus was just awful. I wanted to create a good entry, and maintain a compact academic core." Gordon also wanted to honor the plan set out by the legendary firm. He proposed celebrating the boulevard, giving it a stronger presence, by making it a tree-lined allée (6.1, 6.2, 6.3). He also proposed augmenting the Olmsted design by building, at the boulevard's approximate midpoint, a three-building arts group. He envisioned an art museum named for architectural history professor Theodore Pritchard, and a fire arts center for the College of Arts and

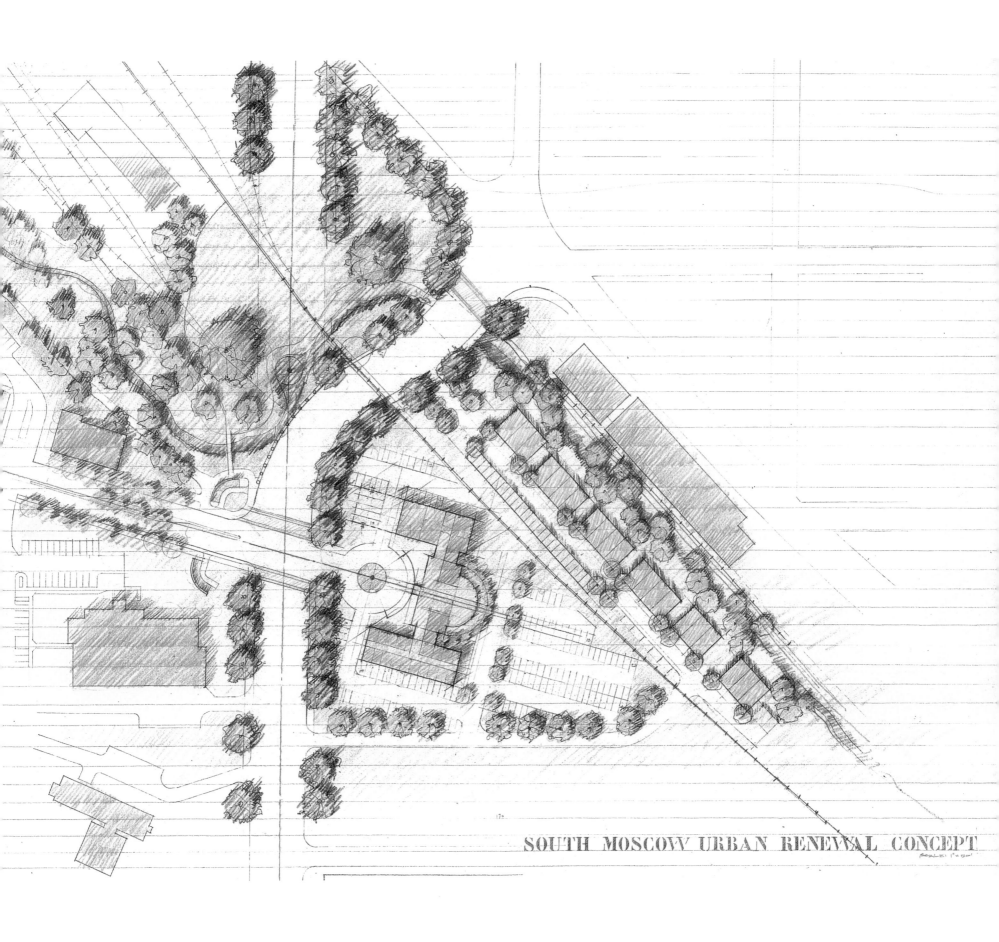

SOUTH MOSCOW URBAN RENEWAL CONCEPT

6.3 César Pelli, schematic design for the Lionel Hampton School of Music, 2003, Moscow, Idaho (unbuilt). Drawing by César Pelli.

6.4 Gordon Walker, Albertson Hall, University of Idaho, Moscow, 1995–97, presentation drawing, "Entry off Circle Drive." The Administration Building is at left. Drawing by Anita Lehmann.

Architecture, both of them focused on the node's major structure, a new music school that would include a large performance auditorium, and would bear Lionel Hampton's name.

Lionel Hampton had performed at the university's jazz festival in 1984. He was impressed by the university's enthusiasm, and pledged his support. The next year's festival was named for him. Two years later—in 1987—the university conferred on him an honorary doctorate, Hampton's eighth, and gave his name to the school of music. With Hampton's name and presence the festival grew to be the largest west of the Mississippi, with as many as 18,000 students gathering in Moscow for sessions all over town, in churches, in schools after hours, in vacant university classrooms. Seizing the obvious, Robert A. Hoover, the university's president, decided to build a curriculum, and a permanent jazz music building, to make the university a national center for jazz study. A state senator with close ties to the university arranged federal funding. Gordon spoke for a national search for an architect, and helped to prepare a program to guide candidates. César Pelli was chosen from an impressive field. He challenged the boulevard site as being too isolated; he wanted to build closer to the campus's core, to better involve the building in university life. Pelli had not been Gordon's first choice for the project, and he regretted the boulevard's loss of the music building, but he found Pelli "a delight to work with," and he agreed that Pelli's argument for location was a sound one. As Pelli developed the design, its strongest element

was the auditorium, whose handsome interior featured a large sliding element to enlarge or reduce the auditorium's size for differing performance needs. The exterior was to be distinguished by a dramatic roof of shifting planes, vaguely—very vaguely—suggestive of Sydney's Opera House (6.4). But a new Lionel Hampton School of Music was not to be. Pelli worked on the project for about nine months. Then, yielding to both political and budgetary arguments, the university dismissed Pelli and shelved the project—and that was the end of it.

By 1992, although Gordon would continue to do projects for California clients, the center of gravity of his practice had shifted to the Northwest. He brought the office back to Seattle that summer, though Colin stayed in California. Gordon brought, too, Sandie Pope, newfound friend, and more than friend—"kind eyes and a big spirit." They started an office together. And they were married December 4, 1992, at one of Ellsworth Storey's picnic shelters on Orcas Island. In California Sandie had been doing interior design work for Gap, the clothing manufacturer. In Seattle she began a consulting practice in retail design, then accepted a position with NBBJ, then with Callison Architects. Gordon taught a design studio at Washington that fall quarter, and continued his architectural practice as in the California office, and under the same name—and he continued work on the Campus Development Plan for his alma mater. Architect Colleen Miller, wife of Gordon's friend and bookdealer Peter Miller, joined the firm.

6.5 Gordon Walker, Albertson Hall, University of Idaho, 1994. Photograph by Andrew van Leeuwen.

6.6 Albertson Hall, and the corner of the Administration Building. Albertson's steeply sloped gable above the entrance, and the concrete glacis in the brick piers, are a nod to the vaguely Collegiate Gothic buildings on the campus, including the adjacent Administration Building. Photograph by Andrew van Leeuwen.

6.7 Gordon Walker, the Jensen Meleliot house, Seattle, 1995, from the east. Photograph by Andrew van Leeuwen.

Joanne Reece, Assistant Vice President for Facilities, was the originating and continuing force behind the Idaho master plan; she had started discussions with Gordon when he was still in California, and before Hoover became president at Moscow. When the plan was nominally complete she asked Gordon to continue to help the school in visualizing aspects of it, and to help them come up with some of their immediate needs as well. Gordon recalls:

This is when I understood the importance of "visual notetaking." Others talk about that kind of thing, but few provide the visualization of what is being considered. It is my notion and I stick with it because it is what I like to do—so that is my focus. I was to investigate the site, the budget, and the program, and translate my conclusions into a story that could be visualized, to move it forward, which it did. I became a very active design consultant, and remained so throughout.

"Visualizing" ultimately meant developing designs for a new student commons, a teaching and learning center, student housing, and an Albertson Building. Gordon had grown to respect YGH —Youst, Grube, Hall—of Portland. Together they submitted a proposal for the Albertson Building, and were selected to design the project, Gordon in the role of Design Coordinator. The building, the first major new structure on the campus in recent times, bears the name of the major donors, Albertson food stores. The most notable building on the campus at the time was the Administration Building, built in 1906 in brick with stone trim, in a Collegiate Medieval style. Its broad façade faced the long curve of the campus entrance drive. From each side of the façade block a wing extended rearward, making the plan a U-shape, with the open side of the U toward the rear. Gordon remembers wondering, in his student days, how he would fit something into the U. Now Albertson Hall was to be sited there, to be a new home for the School of Business (6.5). Gordon saw the building as an opportunity to transform a lost space into an active hub at the center of the campus, while extending the design richness of the Administration Building into that center (6.6).

In 1995 Gordon also designed the Jensen Meleliot residence in Seattle's Madrona neighborhood (6.7);[30] it was a more minor project, but of interest for its relationship to context. The program was modest, but the lot is narrow; the requisite square footage necessitated a four-story tower. Gordon attempted to blend the design with the neighborhood's traditional two-story houses by minimizing floor-to-floor dimensions, therefore overall height, and by echoing the neighborhood's typical gabled roofs and dormers—although two houses by Wendell Lovett, one his own, with neither gabled roofs nor dormers, are just the other side of the street.[31]

In 1996, with the vice chancellor of design construction, Rebekah Gladson, Gordon completed a plan, and a proposal for a seven-story Medical Center, for the University of California at

6.8 Gordon Walker, University of California Irvine campus, conceptual master plan, 1996. The pool at the intersection of the axes is at center, the proposed Medical Center is at top. Drawing by Gordon Walker.

6.9 Cal Irvine, the interior axis and the proposed Medical Center. Drawing by Gordon Walker.

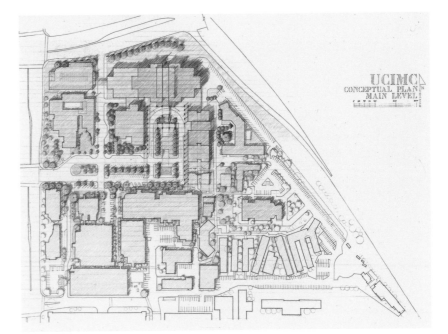

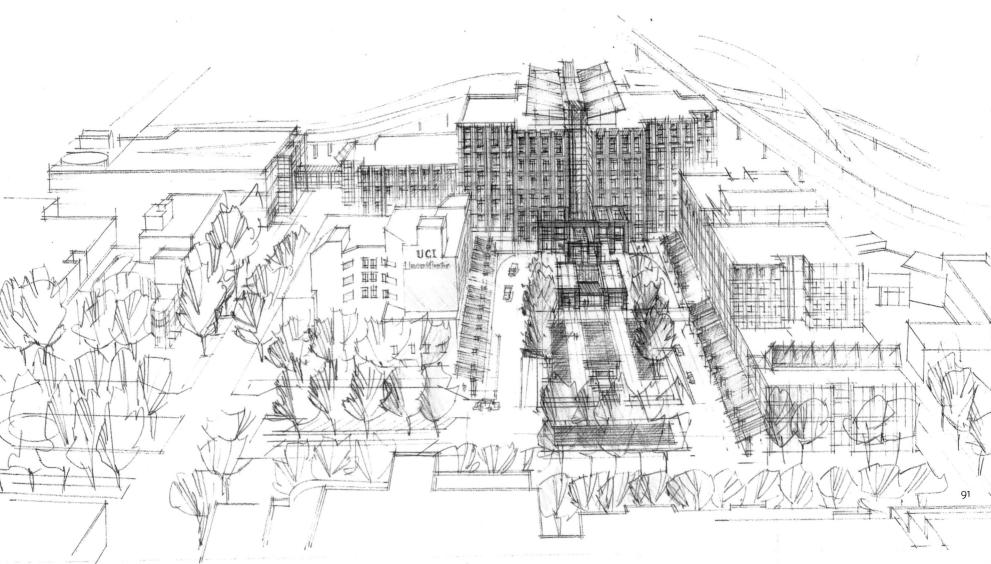

91

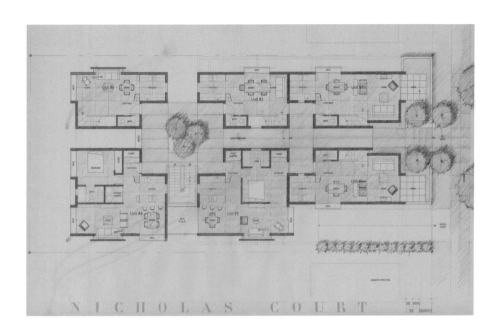

N I C H O L A S   C O U R T

6.10 Gordon Walker, Nicholas Court, Seattle, Washington, 1997: the street façade. Entry to the building's pedestrian walk is at center, the walk is open to the sky between the lower edges of the roof slopes. The descending garage entry is off camera at left. Photograph by Andrew van Leeuwen.

6.11 Nicholas Court, Seattle, Washington, 1997. Plan drawing by Colin Walker.

Irvine (6.8, 6.9). The plan proposed a tree-lined cul-de-sac terminating in a pool that sets up a second axis terminating in the center. Rachel King joined the firm in that year.

In that same year Gordon and Peter Erickson, with the financial backing of Michael Conte, codeveloped a property they had acquired, on which they wanted to build a nine-unit apartment building with required underground parking. The site is very narrow for such a program. Given its tightness, the obvious approach would have been to cover it with units built to lot lines on all sides to maximize rentable square footage, each unit then having two exterior walls, with entry doors on two or four façades, parking underground. Instead, Gordon created pedestrian walkways, micro-streets, that bisect the site on both axes, and intersect in a micro-commons (6.10–6.13). The disadvantages of this idea, and they are large ones, lie in the first expense, and the maintenance, of eight additional exterior walls, and, equally important, the loss of rentable square footage in units that would be small in any case. But the idea gives each unit four exterior walls rather than two; one enters the heart of the complex before entering one's own individual unit. And the walkways and their intersection create a tiny and charmingly maze-like micro-city, something, almost, from a fairy tale, each unit a Hobbit's dwelling. The interiors are remarkable for the satisfying quality of their small spaces, augmented by the spatial release of the patios (6.14, 6.15, 6.16).

On its completion in 1997 Gordon and Sandie moved into Nicholas Court; they would live there until 2004. In October of 1997 Colin moved from California to rejoin the firm. He was accompanied by Kelly Rodriguez, who came along with some reluctance; as a dedicated Californian, she thought Seattle was dogsled territory.[32] She and Colin married in September of 1999.

Pat and Jane Rogers also moved into Nicholas Court on the building's completion in 1997. The following year Gordon designed a house for them,[33] built three years later, for an east-facing waterfront site on Lopez Island. The design for their Lopez site is easy

93

6.12 Nicholas Court, the longer street at twilight. Photograph by Andrew van Leeuwen.

6.13 Nicholas Court, a diagrammatic drawing by Bill Hook.

6.14 Nicholas Court, stair from the
living-dining spaces. Photograph by
Ben Benschneider.

6.15 Nicholas Court, third-floor
stair landing. Photograph by Ben
Benschneider.

6.16 Nicholas Court, a living room.
Photograph by Ben Benschneider.

6.17 Gordon Walker, the Jane and Pat Rogers house, Lopez Island, Washington, 1997; from the southeast. The roofline can be seen sloping away to the west. The dining peninsula is the white volume projecting left—south—with its trellised terrace. The bedroom is above; its deck is the roof of the dining space. Beyond is the small second building of the project. Photograph by Andrew van Leeuwen.

6.18 The Rogers house, the southern dining room terrace. Photograph by Andrew van Leeuwen.

6.19 The Rogers house from the northwest. Photograph by Andrew van Leeuwen.

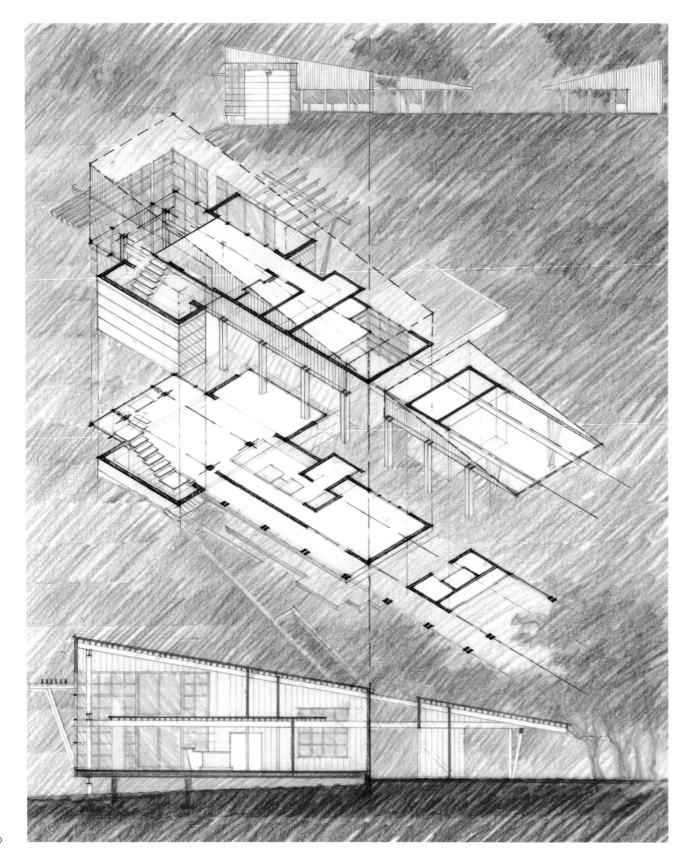

6.20 The Rogers house, section and diagrammatic isometric by Bill Hook.

6.21 The Rogers house; the sitting space, looking toward the Strait of Juan de Fuca. Photograph by Andrew van Leeuwen.

6.22 The Rogers house; the sitting and dining spaces, with Gordon and Pat in dining. One of the paired beams supporting the bedroom is overhead. Photograph by Andrew van Leeuwen.

to describe in its overall form. The exterior is a wedge-like volume, two stories at the east end, one story to the west, apparently transfixed by a two-story element near the east end (6.17, 6.18). There is a service court with shower, west of midway. Farther west, the building ends in a one-car carport whose roof is an eight-foot cantilever (6.19).

The interior of the wedge east of the little shower void includes a guest room, kitchen (6.20), powder room, and a casual living space Gordon has called sitting. The western part of the guest room opens to the roof; a loft hovers above the eastern part. The room opens to the loggia through French doors. The sitting space (6.21) opens laterally to dining space in the transverse element's peninsula (6.22, 6.23), the dining space then opens through more French doors to a trellised terrace (6.17, 6.18). On the other side of the wedge a micro-library is nestled behind a stair (6.24). The stair winds up through 180 degrees to a bedroom (6.25) that overlooks the sitting space and opens, via sliding glass doors, to a terrace over the dining peninsula. A bath and dressing room are to the west. The stair and the dining space are bounded by opaque surfaces, the stair on three sides, dining on two. Short wing walls imply a fourth bounding side for the stair, a third side for dining.

The wedge is nominally[34] sixteen feet wide. Four feet inboard of each long exterior wall are two 4 by 12s spaced three inches apart, so these paired beams are approximately eight feet from each other. Two pairs are horizontal; these support the upper floor (6.21). Two pairs of 4 by 10s, also spaced three inches apart and four feet inboard of the outer walls, support the roof and therefore slope at the roof's angle (6.26). The upper sloping pairs and the lower horizontal pairs intersect at the edge of the carport, where they are notched into one another. These four paired beams determine all major longitudinal interior walls. The northern set also determines the back wall of the loggia and the shower beyond the service court.

Where the horizontal pairs span the sitting space, they support the bedroom floor above. That floor ends about eight feet

6.23 The Rogers house; the kitchen. Just right off the kitchen, beyond the coats, at the farthest point of the image, the French doors from the guest room to the loggia can just be seen. Photograph by Andrew van Leeuwen.

6.24 The Rogers house; the stair and micro-library. The kitchen is off-camera at left, the end of one of the sitting-space sofas is at lower right. The ancestor of the elegantly distinctive lowest step of the stair is at Alvar Aalto's Villa Mairea. Photograph by Andrew van Leeuwen.

from the eastern glass wall. The beams continue, through thin air, as it were, to within six inches of the glass. They are bolted there to steel columns that rise to moment-resisting connections with a beam under the roof, forming a rigid frame that resists lateral forces (6.21, 6.25).

These interior beams are not essential to a sound structure; joists alone could span the sixteen feet; a beam would then be needed only between the sitting and dining spaces. But such joists would be larger in width and depth. Gordon wanted to avoid the real and visual weight, and the beam pairs made that possible. He wanted them too for their sense of strength, and for the order they establish; he concedes that those are the real reasons for their presence. For the beams, and their relationship to the outer walls, establish a symmetry (6.21), or the sense thereof, for the sitting space. That space opens laterally to the dining area that is also symmetrical (6.22), and genuinely so. The bedroom above is also symmetrical if one equates both recesses inboard of the exterior walls (6.20, 6.25). But they can't quite be equated: the recess opposite the stair is habitable; the recess at the stair head is a void. The order of the design, strong and clear, controls a fascinating complexity.

The design was intended to include a complementary structure, a smaller wedge, aligned with the house and with a roof of opposite but identical slope. The two elements imply what, decades earlier, would have been called a butterfly roof (6.17, 6.26). The added element is not an equal success.

Michael Conte had arranged the financing that made Nicholas Court possible. In 1998 Gordon designed a home in Seattle for Michael and Annie; in 1999 he designed a second one, to be built on a craggy waterfront site on Lopez Island (6.27, 6.28). Both crag and house would be dominated by a 130-foot-long concrete thing, a term for which doesn't immediately suggest itself. Gordon and Michael will call it a wall, but since the fairly regular voids are larger than the fairly regular solids, "colonnade" seems closer

6.25 The Rogers house; the head of the stair, the entry to the bedroom. At left, one of the dominant longitudinal paired beams connects to the steel portal. The bedroom is symmetrical if one equates both recesses inboard of the exterior walls. But they can't quite be equated: The recess opposite the stair is habitable; the recess here, at the stair head, is a void. Photograph by Andrew van Leeuwen.

6.26 The Rogers house; the second building. Photograph by Andrew van Leeuwen.

6.27 The second house for Michael and Annie Conte, Lopez Island, 1995–2000. The exterior from the east. The dominant wall is at the far left, the kitchen can be seen through the second bay. The steel frame with its angled strut can be seen through the glass of the "sitting space" at center. The bedroom peninsula is beyond; the master bedroom is at extreme right. Photograph by Andrew van Leeuwen.

6.28 The Conte house: site plan and plan. The dominant wall or colonnade is the series of heavy dashed lines. Major spaces lie above it in this drawing, kitchen and terrace below. Drawing by Gordon Walker.

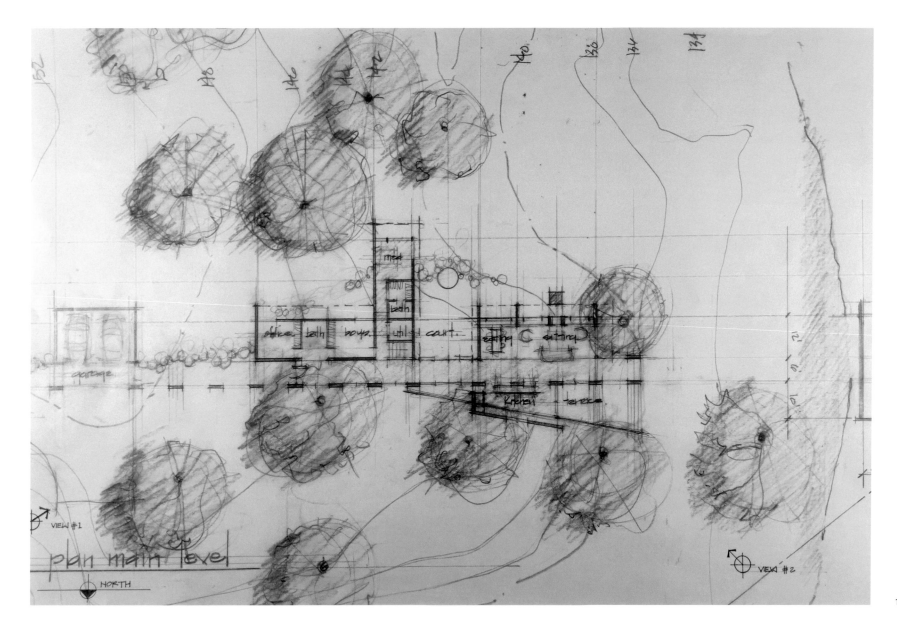

6.29 The Conte house; sitting space at left, kitchen at right. Photograph by Andrew van Leeuwen.

to the mark. It is oriented northwest to southeast. Gordon said: "Standing on the property, the line of the wall drew itself."

On the ferry from Lopez back to Seattle Gordon and Michael worked out the rudiments of a design. The concrete colonnade would be the organizing element, all spaces emerging from it. Materials would be hard-edged, industrial—floors of concrete, possibly concrete kitchen counters, entirely steel structure above including ceilings, no re-sawn cedar anywhere, steel and concrete all exposed. These decisions may have been suggested by Michael Conte; certainly he approved them. He had a deep-running enthusiasm for the new, the technically advanced, the daring, and he accompanied this enthusiasm with a tremendous, untiring energy. He said to Gordon: "Let's do it."[35]

The colonnade extends northwest beyond the corridor it edges to front a pending garage, and extends free to the southeast (6.28). All living spaces except the kitchen and its terrace are northeast of the corridor. The outer edges of those spaces are defined by various concrete walls and piers. All but the boys' room and the office have views of the Strait of Juan de Fuca; the master bedroom (6.31) and the "sitting space" (6.29) have stunning 90-degree views of it, from northeast to southeast. A court at midpoint offers shelter from the winds that beset the island; a patio beyond, open to the winds, commands a sweeping outlook to the strait. The kitchen and its terrace southwest of the corridor have only bits of view here and there, filtered through the trees and undergrowth of a dense wood (6.28).

The superstructure throughout is of steel. Frames of sloped roofs northeast of the corridor are braced by steel struts perpendicular to the roof's slope (6.30). The sloped roofs create clerestories that bring southern light into all of these spaces except those leading to the master bedroom; their clerestory faces northeast.[36]

In 1994 Gordon had designed a PNB practice facility in Bellevue. It was demolished in 2016 for yet another design by Gordon with Mithun, on the same site, this one a straightforward

6.30 The Conte house; looking toward the sitting space from the dining space. Photograph by Andrew van Leeuwen.

6.31 The Conte house: the master bedroom; the Strait of Juan de Fuca is in view through the windows at extreme right. Photograph by Andrew van Leeuwen.

6.32, 6.33 The original Francia Russell Center in Bellevue, Washington, 2000. Photographs by Steve Ringman, the *Seattle Times*.

practice facility built as the Pacific Northwest Ballet School, and named the Francia Russell Center (6.32, 6.33). At the same time Gordon designed a house for Kent and Francia on Whidbey Island (6.34–6.38), that is an exquisite elaboration of the Rogers wedge.

In 2003, among many other projects, Gordon designed an extensive remodel of the DeLaurenti Deli in the Pike Place Market. The following year he had more work than he could handle; inevitably this meant a lot of delegating, to Colleen, Colin, Rachel, and Robert May. His own time was increasingly spent in management. He decided, yet again, that, "My skills were in design and building, not business management. I was sixty-five, and I wanted a change. We all finished what we were doing, everybody found another job, and we closed the door. It took six months to close things up, and during that time I once again pondered my future. If I really wanted no more of independent practice, I had to find a firm in which I could just design."

6.34 The Kent Stowell and Francia Russell house, Whidbey Island, 2000: the façade toward the water. The higher landward volume is just visible beyond. Photograph by Andrew van Leeuwen.

6.35 The Stowell-Russell house, from the entry court: the Rogers wedge elaborated. This view is misleading in suggesting that the roofs lie in the same plane; see figs. 6.34, 6.38. Photograph by Andrew van Leeuwen.

6.36 The Stowell-Russell house, dining space. Kitchen is at right, living space left, with the study beyond. Photograph by Andrew van Leeuwen.

6.37 The Stowell-Russell house, the study beyond the living space; the bookshelves wall echoes the larger spatial articulation seen in fig. 6.36. Photograph by Andrew van Leeuwen.

6.38 The Stowell-Russell house.
Photograph by Andrew van Leeuwen.   113

7 GORDON AT MITHUN

DAVE GOLDBERG   BRENDAN CONNOLLY

OMER MITHUN RECEIVED a Bachelor of Architecture degree from the University of Minnesota in 1942, and a degree in naval architecture from the University of Michigan in 1945. He came west to Bremerton to work briefly in the naval shipyards, then to Seattle to work for Naramore, Bain, Brady, and Johanson until 1949. In that year he began a storefront architectural practice in Bellevue, and an assistant professorship at the University of Washington. His practice prospered, he won many awards, was elected to the AIA's College of Fellows in 1973, and was promoted to full professor at the university in 1982, in later years teaching classes in passive energy-conserving design, on which he had become an expert. On his death in 1983 he left a solid and thriving, highly respected firm. Mithun Partners moved from Bellevue to the Times Square Building in the heart of Seattle in 1988, then, in 2000, to Pier 56 on the Seattle waterfront, practicing thereafter as simply Mithun (7.1, 7.2). The firm has always had the highest of reputations, and as a consequence has prospered and grown. There is now a satellite Mithun office in San Francisco, and the Seattle office comprises about 150 architects, landscape architects, land use planners, and interior designers, working under the grand wooden structure of the turn-of-the-century pier. From a field of hundreds of firms, Mithun received the 2017 AIA Northwest and Pacific Firm Award.

Gordon closed Walker Architecture in 2004 not because he had tired of architecture but because he had tired of the business of architecture. Fortunately for both himself and Mithun, his son Colin introduced him to Ron van der Veen, who helped set up an interview with Bert Gregory, then Mithun's CEO, and Dave Goldberg, one of Gordon's former University of Washington students. With an eye toward continuing to grow the quality of the practice, they quickly realized Gordon's potential impact, and offered him a position as a Consulting Principal, a title he still holds today. He was invited to design smaller projects, to lead design teams on larger scale work, and to mentor younger architects within the firm. The agreement was that he would work thirty hours a week

7.1 Gordon and two Mithun designers shaping a project, 2018. Photograph: Mithun.

7.2 Mithun, the office in the heavy-timber structure of Pier 56, looking transversely. Photograph by Juan Hernandez.

for one year. One year became two, then three, then everybody stopped counting. Gordon said:

> This suited my independent nature perfectly, and thirteen-plus years later, it still works with no revisits to the original hand-shake. I was interested in Mithun because of their interest in developing a fully integrated design firm that focused on sustainable and biophilic[37] design. They have been very good for me. Over the years I learned that there was a way to continue to be useful—to learn and grow. I've always been interested in reinventing my particular talent and passion for design that focuses on today's needs.

Gordon has brought to Mithun an innate and unqualified commitment to elegant design solutions, and an equally deep commitment to the people around him. He has thrived at the firm with this balance of devotion to design and to people—much in the spirit of Omer Mithun. Gordon's personal ethos was so completely aligned with the office's past and present that it would have been hard to make it not work. He has entrenched himself as an irreplaceable part of the firm's spirit, influencing generations of designers with his rigor, his passion, the sheer quality of his designs, and the gentle humor of his critical style (7.1).

It is nearly impossible to separate Gordon's work from his personal relationships with the firm, the community, and the clients that have surrounded him at Mithun. He has not only inspired so many of us to be better at our craft, but also to value the people we work for and with. We are a practice in which ideas have always outweighed egos, and this can be said of Gordon as well. His roll of yellow trace has landed on scores of desks at the firm (7.2), and those lucky enough be at those desks, to work directly with him, are never quite the same; they are inspired—perhaps exhausted—by the questions he wasn't invited to ask, maybe still smiling about the joke with which he wandered away.

7.3 The Mithun office, looking toward Elliott Bay, with a ferry in view on its way to Bainbridge Island. Photograph by Juan Hernandez.

7.4 Gordon dispensing his sage input on his signature yellow trace, 2018. Photograph by Juan Hernandez.

When Gordon joined the firm in 2004, the understanding was that he would himself design small-scale projects, and would assist with larger projects in what he has described as a "player-coach" role (7.3, 7.4). Since that time he has contributed to projects over a tremendous range of scales and typologies. In a typical week he may be designing high-rise residential towers, tech offices in Silicon Valley, perhaps a facility for a university. At this writing, Gordon has accrued over 17,000 hours in transforming scores of projects as "player-coach," while also leading the design of several notable projects in which he is properly credited with authorship. Gordon's experience and passion for housing especially has influenced multiple urban housing projects, in the physical context of buildings and urban design, and in the quality of the individual human experience.

Domaine was his first assignment at Mithun (7.5). Gordon's task was to make sense of a mixed residential project that straddles a challenging sloping site on the east side of Seattle's Queen Anne Hill. The site is bounded on one side by the very heavily trafficked Aurora Avenue corridor where it approaches the bridge over the Fremont cut, and on the other side by a view of limitless reach, over Lake Union and to the Cascade Mountains beyond. Beginning his design explorations in concert with the client and the team, Gordon quickly realized both the challenge and the energy of the site. He created a massing that offers a rhythmic edge to the speeding cars along Aurora, a staggered linear façade that is scaled to the speed and energy of the automobile. He coupled this with a protected mews and interior residential spaces that afford residents sanctuary and a prospect from which to enjoy the majestic view. The project created a dynamic edge to the Aurora corridor, experienced by many millions of residents of this region, and also a comfortable dwelling that several Mithun employees have since elected to call home.

Over his career, Gordon has continuously sought to go beyond what he has done before, with a particular interest in how things get built. Many at Mithun share this same commitment, reinventing perfectly suitable solutions in search of something new, smarter, often more difficult—for which Gordon's drive to innovate is a perfect match.

His work on the Unico properties prefabricated modular prototype illustrates his habit of pushing his own thinking, challenging the design and construction industries to learn and grow as well. The project that emerged at Mithun in 2007 was a collaboration with Unico Properties to design and build a prototype prefabricated unit for urban housing, entitled "Inhabit," to test new possibilities for realizing compact urban living space (7.6). Gordon worked hand in hand with a small project team, leading them into the fine art of ignoring the costs, loving a project to death, creating a unit that could be built rapidly, with the cost savings of factory production,

7.5 Mithun, Gordon Walker, project
lead designer, Domaine, Seattle,
2005. The view from Aurora. Photos
Ben Benschneider.

7.6 Mithun, Gordon Walker, designer
in collaboration with HyBrid and
Unico Properties. "Inhabit" prototype
modular dwelling unit, Seattle, 2007.
Photograph by Juan Hernandez.

7.7 Mithun, Gordon Walker, key design team member, Press Blocks mixed-use development, 2005, Portland, Oregon. Photograph by Plompmozes.

without sacrificing design quality and livability. What emerged was a seminal idea in urban architecture, a prototypical dwelling of modest proportions, its interior akin to a well-designed boat in its efficiency of space, in which every cubic inch elegantly fulfills its purpose.

This project was an important stimulus to Mithun's work in research and development. The firm is currently exploring cross-laminated timber structures for high-rise housing, advanced means for prefabrication that employ cutting-edge industrial processes, and means for advanced energy performance. Gordon has brought a renewed vigor to our commitment to innovation that must be rigorous and uncompromising in its design integrity.

Gordon's interest in urban housing has also found its way to recent works in Portland. He has been a key member of the design teams for several mixed-use housing and office developments, including Block 136 and Press Blocks, two projects with

high-rise residential towers, retail and office uses, and public exterior spaces (7.7–7.11). Gordon cited "integrated disciplines and thinking" as one of his reasons for coming to the firm. In the face of significant zoning and regulatory pressures, these projects are inspired examples of blended outdoor and indoor spaces in dense urban environments, while Gordon's attention to materiality and tectonics are evident in the brick and steel detailing. Contextual, modern, and timeless, these projects seamlessly merge with the fabric of Portland's character.

Mithun had developed over the years a systematic design process. Deep programmatic, site, and environmental analyses were typically followed by deliberate testing of multiple design schemes at increasingly larger scales, from interiors to building form to urban design. Gordon, on the other hand, works at the macro and micro

7.8 Mithun, Gordon Walker, contributing designer, Block 136 mixed-use paired building masses, Portland, Oregon, 2008–10. Rendering by Mir.

scales simultaneously, arriving at a poetry of built form, as the simultaneous explorations at varying scales meld. In many cases, Gordon has engaged with teams who, part way through the design process, were mired in design options and looking for some clarity in order to move effectively forward. Roll of trace and pencil in hand, he would talk to the team, start laying out structural grids, building sections, even material details, bringing cohesive thinking to the table, getting the team to move quickly beyond diagrams to more fully comprehending a logical path ahead.

In one memorable instance, Gordon joined a team designing a large resort and spa, as the team were trying to resolve major issues of building elevations and massing. He showed up at his first meeting with the client holding a piece of cedar siding, with two cans of stain, and proceeded to talk about ways to mix the stains to create a weathered look that would work with the muted colors of the rolling grassy hills around the site. The client and team were

7.9 Block 136, pedestrian alley: integrated landscape and architectural space. Rendering by Mir.

7.10 Entry lobby and stair with acoustic lighting sculpture. Photograph by Kevin Scott.

7.11 Aerial view of three interconnected program elements: the office building, public courtyard, and residential tower. Photograph by Kevin Scott.

7.12 One of the cool kids: Gordon behind virtual reality goggles during a design session. Photograph: Mithun.

7.13 The player-coach: Gordon on a UC San Diego project critique in Mithun's Seattle Pier 56 office, 2017. Photograph: Mithun.

7.14 Mithun, Gordon Walker, contributing designer, Cross-Laminated Timber Student Housing Prototype, 2011, in collaboration with Katerra. Rendering by Plompmozes.

surprised by the change in discussion, and didn't know why he was promoting stain colors when there were clearly bigger decisions to make. But by jump-starting the conversation with the scale of the detail, Gordon was able to help the team understand the aesthetic and technical implications of the larger moves, thereby creating an integrated and logical step forward with the design.

While Gordon could easily claim full credit for his design leadership on many of the projects where he has contributed, this has never been his style. He is immune to praise, seeks no attribution—he thrives on the success of the emerging talent around him (7.12, 7.13). On Block 136 he managed to find an influential yet humble position on the project team, providing guidance and design inspiration, but constantly empowering the next generations of designers and architects, making them feel that the building belongs to them, is their creation. Greg Catron, one of the emerging young architects at Mithun, spent numerous hours working with Gordon on Block 136, and recalls his modesty and grace in this effort:

Despite his legendary status, his approachability is unparalleled. I remember one experience early in my career in which I had to present my work to Gordon and several others I look up to. Their feedback left me a little lost, second-guessing my approach. I came to Gordon to request further feedback, and he was excited to dive deeper into the work. He pushed me to keep following my path, and in the end, I was very proud of what I'd done. I don't

know that I would have ended up there without his willingness to listen and offer guidance.

As with anyone who has a storied career, he represents a wealth of experience that is always informing our work as a firm, and I find that his collaboration brings a distinctive level of humanity to our projects.

Emily Hagen, another rising architect at the firm, writes of her first week at Mithun, and the words of wisdom from the veterans: "The first piece of advice I was given was to latch on to Gordon and soak up every piece of advice, every story he tells, and to save all his sketches."

Emily and Gordon later collaborated on another innovative high-rise design concept for student housing using prefabrication and cross-laminated timber (7.14). This effort reflects Gordon's passion for learning innovative ways to exploit new construction technologies, and his life-long fascination with wood as a fundamental building material in his native Northwest.

If we were to sort out participants in the firm's design crits over the past decade, Gordon's track record would stand above the rest. Sometimes sweet, often salty, always straightforwardly candid, usually laser-focused, his critiques are driven by an urge to help others be their best as well as to continue his own design growth. His own reflection on his time at Mithun is concise and accurate: "Over the past fourteen years as a consultant, I have learned that the younger designers in the firm become my clients

123

7.15 The new Francia Russell Center, Bellevue, WA. Photograph by Kevin Scott.

and my connection to the profession. I think of it as learning from teaching or, as I think of it, a passion for design, how to learn from the next generation and still be rather subjective."

While Gordon has asked to be less client-facing at this stage of his career, his commitment to mentoring younger staff at Mithun is rivaled, nevertheless, by his commitment to the clients he works with. He recently led the design of a new Francia Russell ballet center in Bellevue, a modest renovation to create a new school and program space for the Pacific Northwest Ballet (7.15). Completed in 2017, this new facility brings Gordon full circle, to a reprise of his work for the ballet's founders decades before. The new project's simple lines, humble materials, and thoughtful composition serve as a perfect backdrop for students and performers who use this space. Chip Hammer, project architect at Mithun, recalls observing Gordon through this process:

What struck me the most in my time working with Gordon was his commitment to the client. For many architects of Gordon's generation, clients were a means to an end, an avenue to getting their creative expression built — Gordon, quite the opposite. Keeping the trust and developing genuine relationships with the client was paramount for Gordon. He shared several stories with me about his time as a young architect, including how much time he spent building the projects he designed. He built them knowing it would be more affordable for the client, allowing them to actually get the home they desired. It was this sweat equity that has endeared Gordon to so many people, and what I view as a major part of his success…not drawing anything he wouldn't be willing to build himself.

Many at Mithun aspire to have as much "street cred" as Gordon does with all members of the firm. He moves whatever he must in his personal schedule, with his wife, Sandie, and his island goats, to make himself available for project meetings; to take an emerging professional to coffee, lunch, dinner or a hike around his property; to talk about project issues, design problems, and individual career goals. His personality is infectious. So many of us are humbled by his presence, peering over his glasses at a desk where he never turns his back, intently studying the tail of his roll of yellow trace, warmly eager to engage with anyone who approaches him, at any hour.

In 2007, early in the throes of the design for the Nordic Heritage Museum in the Ballard neighborhood (7.16, 7.17), Gordon offered a client new to Seattle a tour of Lake Washington and the Ballard Locks, to view the project site and its larger context

from the water. On a rainy Saturday morning, the client and the project team came to Gordon's boat slip to enjoy an extraordinary outpouring of hospitality. They gathered in and on the 34-foot 1930s wooden powerboat, all brass and mahogany, that Gordon had spent two years restoring and, on occasion, had lived aboard. Gordon had prepared a buffet for the occasion—oysters, calamari, smoked salmon, mussels, bread from The Bakery, and a sampling of Aquavit contributed by Juhani Pallasmaa, friend from Finland and collaborating design architect. With everyone fed or feeding, Gordon spoke for a while on Seattle's water history. Then, the water tour. It gave everyone a new perspective of the site, and it set a lasting tone of friendship and shared quest between client and design team. This kind of gesture, free of pretention, affectation, or arrogance, transparent in its warmth, is Gordon.

Since the completion in 2007 of his inspirational cabin on Orcas, scores of young and old Mithun souls have trekked to the island to camp out in the guest tent, feed the goats, sit by the fire with Gordon and Sandie, laughing over a glass of wine and a Gordon-cooked meal. Unforgettable hours.

In poring through the earlier pages of this manuscript, we were not surprised to find that Gordon had once been the youngest licensed fly-fishing guide in Idaho. The poetics and

7.16 Mithun, The New Nordic Heritage Museum, Ballard, Seattle, Washington, 2018. This design is indicative of the quality of the firm's work; Gordon played only a minor role in the design. Image by Mir.

7.17 The New Nordic Heritage Museum, the lobby. Image by Mir.

mechanics of tying and casting an artificial fly require a mastery of the intimate detail, and a love of the larger landscape. There are lessons in humility and patience in the casting and waiting—and euphoria as the brown trout, from its deep refuge, rises to close on the offering. But as a guide, this euphoria was not Gordon's to achieve. His task was to lead others to the euphoria. In doing so, Gordon would have revealed an innate understanding of people, of how to teach and how to lead. By just a bit of a stretch, one could suggest an analogy between Gordon as fishing guide and Gordon at Mithun: he is quick to see an opportunity and its potential outcome, but refrains from reaching for it himself, he empowers others to do so. So he develops in future generations of architects the ability to cast their lines with confidence and success. We feel lucky to have him among us.

8 A PREFAB ON ORCAS ISLAND

THE SAN JUAN ARCHIPELAGO includes numerous small islands and three major ones: San Juan, Lopez, and Orcas (8.1), which are roughly equal in size. San Juan and Orcas are the more populous; Orcas is the northernmost. Its configuration could be described as three lobes descending southward from a narrow isthmus that is the northern edge of the island. The ferry from Anacortes docks at the town of Orcas, on the southern shore of the island's middle lobe. From the Orcas dock the island's main road runs northward, then, briefly, east, to the charming major town, Eastsound, on the south shore of the isthmus. The road then continues east and south along the eastern lobe to Moran State Park, which includes Mount Constitution, the highest point in the islands; the state park lake surrounded by buildings designed by Seattle architect Ellsworth Storey (8.2, 8.3); and the Rosario resort, originally the Moran mansion.

In the early 2000s Gordon and Sandie Pope bought a ten-acre tract on Orcas, west of the Orcas-Eastsound road, half a mile west of Eastsound. Sandie loves animals, wanted to raise some, llamas, maybe goats. She saw the Orcas property as a good place to raise them. Gordon is conscious of advancing years; he has a growing interest in senior housing. "I can't find anything in the senior realm that I'd consider dying in, let alone living in." He thought the idea of a factory-built prefabricated house that had been taken some way at Mithun was worth exploring further. As the idea developed, he realized the value of building a prototype. In 2006 he built his cabin on the Orcas site.

The modern history of the prefabricated building goes back to at least the California Gold Rush; it attracted prefabs as large as the four-story Graham Hotel. They came from Chicago and New York in wood, and from England in iron; wooden prefabs from China included a carpenter to assemble them. In the 1930s Walter Gropius and Konrad Wachsmann, working in London until the obviously pending war, then in the United States, designed a metal house of great sophistication and beauty.[38]

8.1 Orcas Island, in the San Juan Islands, seen from the ferry when rounding a promontory of Lopez Island. The highest point on the far horizon is the peak of Mount Constitution in Moran State Park; the lookout tower can just be discerned. Photograph by Grant Hildebrand.

8.2 Ellsworth Storey, picnic shelter at Moran State Park Orcas Island, San Juan Islands, built in the 1930s. Photograph by Grant Hildebrand.

8.3 Storey, Orcas Island picnic shelter, 1930s. Gordon and Sandie were married here, in 1992. Photograph by Grant Hildebrand.

In those same years Buckminster Fuller designed the hexagonal Dymaxion house, then the circular Wichita house, meant to be produced by Beech Aircraft in Wichita. Shortly after World War II Carl Koch at MIT developed the wooden Techbuilt house, and the Aluminum Company of America, ALCOA, developed a range of models in aluminum.

None of this work came into meaningful production. Though they brought immigrant Chinese carpenters to the west coast, the Gold Rush prefabs could not compete with the lightweight frame construction system—the balloon frame—devised in Chicago in 1832, whose progeny still dominate American residential building. Two of the Gropius-Wachsmann houses were built in Haifa at prohibitive expense. Fuller's Wichita house could neither accept expansion nor offer options, it was ill-suited to other than flat sites, and ill-suited too to the rectangular world of appliances, furniture, and rugs; Beech Aircraft returned to making airplanes. A few of the Koch and ALCOA houses were produced; they found no meaningful market. The greatest successes in this sort of thing have been the so-called "double-wides," more or less conventional-looking designs, factory-built in halves to be joined on site, with a wide range of choices and options. Designed for transport, each half is typically ten or eleven feet wide, a common road width limit.

Gordon too began with transport criteria: his design is based on a grid sized to fit anything from a humble flatbed truck upward. The design answers problems of adaptation to site by perching on steel post extensions of the superstructure—"touching the earth lightly," in Glenn Murcutt's phrase (8.4). It touches the earth lightly too because the building itself is light. It is made of ordinary materials: six-lam plywood countertops, high-density fiberboard, vertical-grain fir doors; steel structural frame, concrete floor, wooden decks and entry walk, plate glass walls and windows.

The living room is at one end, the bedroom at the other (8.5–8.7). Between, an island includes kitchen, office/guest room, utilities, and bathrooms. Three conventional wood-frame walls in the island accept plumbing and electrical runs. Glass walls at the ends open the living and dining spaces to the island's forest (8.8, 8.9, 8.10), the bedroom to a small clearing. The linear organization answers the matter of additions by what one might call the "loaf of bread" concept: one adds slices to the loaf, presumably indefinitely, although the realistic limit is probably two bedrooms plus den—beyond that the necessary corridor loses its charm. The steel-frame structure—continuous steel beams linking simple shed-roof frames at sixteen-foot intervals—is visible inside and out. All opaque elements—floor, walls, roof, except only the wooden transverse walls—are "sip" panels, in varying thicknesses sandwiched between varying upper and lower surfaces; the floor's upper surface is a two-inch concrete pour. Above the intermediate horizontal on the north is a continuous clerestory; below is what might be thought of as a continuous architectural saddlebag (8.11, 8.12). It is not, however, an add-on element. It is borne by cantilevered extensions of the floor "sip" panels, so is integral to the design. The saddlebag accommodates the entry (8.6, 8.13–8.17) and storage including closets, and where not serving those purposes it expands the lateral dimension of the interior (8.7, 8.10).

The house was built by assembling complete sixteen-foot modules at the western end. These were then moved eastward, one by one, to their finished locations. In this way the basic house was built in seven days.

Sandie and Gordon have been happy in the house, and it seems a reasonable candidate for prefabrication. It is easy to envision the factory-fabricated steel frame arriving at the site, foundation points connected, the floor poured, factory-built kitchen-bath unit and saddlebag elements arrive and are installed, glass is put in place, the furniture is delivered—the new owner moves in. The house could be ordered as a one-bedroom package, or guest/office and master bedroom, or guest and two bedrooms. Yet the Orcas house too has failed to find a path to actual production.

8.4 Gordon Walker, the Orcas house, Orcas Island, 2006, from the south. The bedroom is at left, the living space at right, perched above the swale. Photograph by Andrew van Leeuwen.

8.5 The Orcas house; the bedroom
terrace, merging with the clearing.
Photograph by Andrew van Leeuwen.

8.6 The Orcas house; the floor plan.

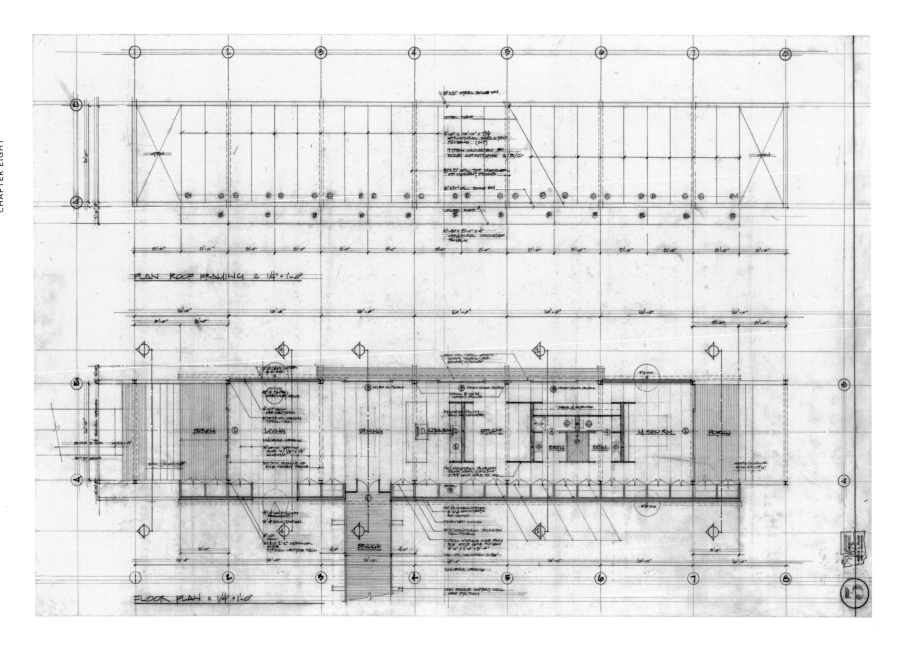

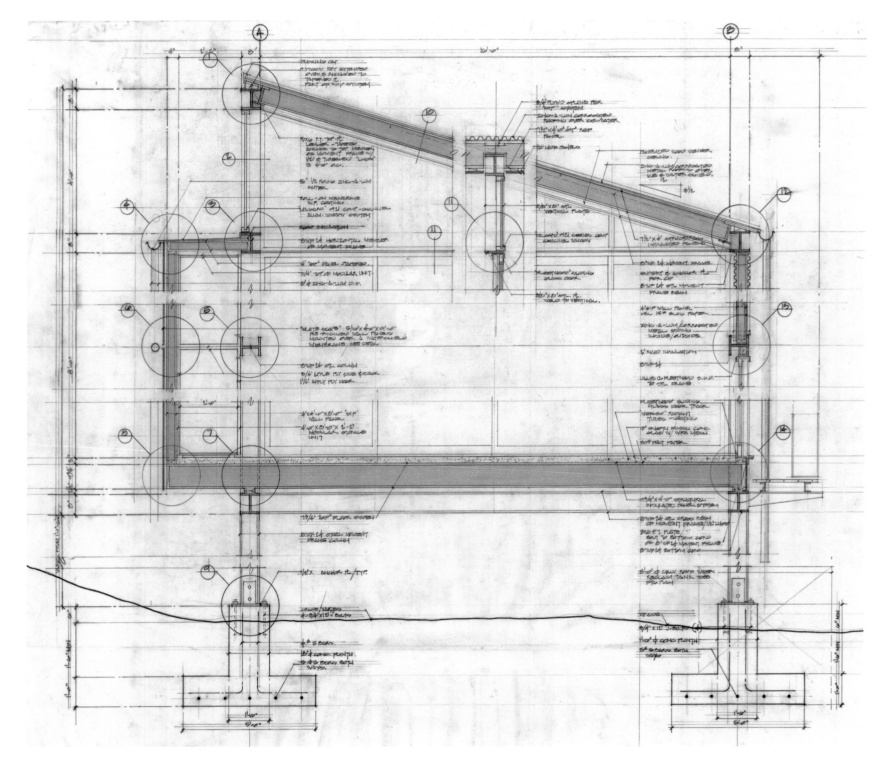

8.8 The Orcas house, touching the earth lightly. Photograph by Grant Hildebrand.

8.9 The Orcas house, the entry. Photograph by Andrew van Leeuwen.

8.10 The Orcas house: The living space, the deck beyond, saddlebag at left, clerestory above; the steel frame evident throughout. Photograph by Ben Benschneider.

8.11 The Orcas house: the east end,
showing the deck structure. Photograph by Andrew van Leeuwen.

8.12 The Orcas house, Gordon and Sandie in the kitchen, the entry is at extreme right. Photograph by Ben Benschneider.

8.13 The Orcas house, the entry walk at twilight. Photograph by Andrew van Leeuwen.

Gordon still wants to design something that will. He hoped it might be a case-study project he developed to be realized on the island. "I've been looking at Eastsound," he says. "Drew up a plan for four modular units in a condo group. The elements would be factory fabricated, off-island, brought in on barges, in boxes. Each unit would be 900 square feet or less and would cost between $350,000 and $375,000. We've got to quit building the memory of what was." But the world he is addressing is not as eager to quit that memory. He has shown his idea to various groups: "the response was near freezing. So far, people don't like them," he says. "They say, 'I want something I recognize.'" Fabrication and erection are one thing, taste is quite another.

8.14 Gordon Walker, a bird feeder, Orcas Island, maybe 2014. Photograph by Andrew van Leeuwen.

8.15 The Orcas house guest tent: an *Architectural Digest* editor studies the structure. Photograph by Michael Burns.

8.16 The Orcas house guest tent: aesthetic pragmatics, elegant rusticity. Photograph by Andrew van Leeuwen.

8.17 The Orcas house, the bedroom deck on a summer evening. Photograph by Andrew van Leeuwen.

9 TEACHER AND MENTOR

GORDON TAUGHT A DESIGN STUDIO on a full-time appointment at the University of Idaho in 1970–71, and part-time at the University of Washington in the fall of 1976, the spring of 1986, and the fall of 1992 and 1998.[39] He has been frequently sought as juror before and during his time at Mithun, and has served as member of four thesis committees, two of which he chaired. And although it isn't exactly mentoring or teaching, it bears mentioning that Gordon was six times asked to serve on American Institute of Architects award juries although he was only briefly a member of the AIA; such was his reputation as critic.

Mithun's officers encouraged these activities, because they meshed with the original understanding that a significant part of Gordon's time would be given to mentoring younger architects in the firm.

Those mentored are seldom aware of the mentoring, because Gordon's methods are invariably clad in the innate and unaffected charm—warmth may be a better word—that has served him so well on so many occasions. Often the mentoring consists of encouragement, a bit of guidance, a sketch or two, a revision or two, help with a critical detail. It is in the nature of the task, however, that occasionally Gordon will completely disagree with the mentored architect's direction. He will then, typically, sit down with that architect, colleague to colleague, to begin, usually, with, "What happens if we come back around…"—no condescension, no confrontation, the conversation always given credence by the record of Gordon's accomplishments, known to all at the office, as they are at school. (One comment about his mentoring at the office, however—"He guides you without doing it for you"—is not entirely true. When Gordon believes a project is fatally off the mark but he cannot lead the project architect toward a fundamentally different direction, he manages to do it his way, usually without visibly seeming to do so.) One of the mentored architects, who chooses to remain anonymous, comments on his experience:

[Gordon] challenges me to make each line meaningful. He teaches without arrogance, allowing dialog and input. He places importance on the soul of a project, reminds me to discover it, not to lose sight of it, and to fight for it. He cares for the quality of design, more passionately than just about anyone else I know; but at bottom of it all, he cares first and foremost about the people he designs for and those he works with. Gordon is one of the true legends in Seattle architecture, a natural mentor to anyone he touches. People working with him feel empowered. Gordon's natural grace and authority bring out the best in people.

Rachel King worked with Gordon for some time, both in his independent practice and at Mithun. Her description of her experience is worth quoting at length:

I met Gordon initially when he came into Sergio Palleroni's studio a few times to give desk critiques. I remember him being insightful and thoughtful as a stranger in the classroom.

I wound up working for him by chance — he was looking for a model builder, and a friend put a note on my desk that said, "Call Gordon Walker he needs a model builder." So I called him and he

9.1 Katie Egland Cox with Gordon Walker, the "Larch" house, Sandpoint, Idaho, 2013–14. The house is entered from the carport. Its ancestry in Gordon's own house on Orcas Island is evident here. Photograph by Andrew van Leeuwen.

9.2 "Larch," with steps to the house. Photograph by Andrew van Leeuwen.

hired me just for one project in spring 1999. I don't think he was looking to grow his office. At the time the only other people were Colin Walker, Colleen Miller, and Robert May. I sat at a desk and built the Judah residence model for a few months, and he sat down next to me one day and asked, "Well, can you draw?" I worked for him through to the closing of the office.

In the office he was an incredible mentor and guide… very generous with his time with regard to explaining detailing.

As an intern working with him I don't remember any of us ever discussing spatial relationships — as a draftsman and detailer I would focus on lining things up (window mullions, structural planes, etc.). I remember visiting the projects and during construction being surprised by the harmonies of the space, as well

9.3 "Larch": the carport, with the roof of the house, parallel in slope, beyond. The structure recalls both the Conte house on Lopez Island and the Walker house on Orcas. Photograph by Andrew van Leeuwen.

as how strong the inside/outside relationships were. I think his concepts were always in three dimensions even when I was not aware of it.... He had a strong vision from the onset for each project I worked on with him.

He seemed to have the design worked out in his head early on. Gordon would meet with the client and walk the site, and come up with sketches—napkin sketches even, in the case of Lopez Island residence. And the final project would very closely resemble these initial concepts despite going through the design development phase.

When he closed the office he took me with him to Mithun as a consultant, which I was so grateful for.

I am very aware of how fortunate I was to fall into my job with Gordon's office. His office felt like family (which when I joined was family, with Colin and Colleen) and he nurtured me as an intern like family. I used to apologize for asking questions and he would say how silly that was. Gordon was incredibly generous with his time, his talent, his home.

Lopez Island was the first project I worked on as a project architect—it was already under construction when I got involved with it, and we went up to the job site every week. The project was a huge puzzle getting the siding boards to align, the seams of the built-ins tracing throughout

I recall once having an "ah-háh" moment standing in the kitchen and looking over the stainless steel island. My eyes connected the plane of the island steel to the steely gray water beyond, and then turning to look out the side window, the concrete benches with their dark green cushions melded into the lichen-covered rocks beyond. A house made of steel and concrete connected so beautifully to its wild surrounding.

Katie Egland Cox was one of those Gordon mentored at the university. She was an outstanding student in the UW graduate architecture program; department chair Vikram Prakash said he

wanted to delay Katie's graduation, indefinitely if possible, because he couldn't see how the department could push on without her. (She graduated nevertheless, in 2012. The department has soldiered on.) Gordon had been her design studio teacher, chair of her thesis committee and, after her graduation, a friend. For eventual professional registration Katie would need three years of internship, to be certified by a registered architect. She wanted to begin her internship by working, with Gordon's guidance, on a home for herself in her native Idaho, the town from whose high school Gordon had graduated fifty-five years earlier, and where his mother still lived. Katie wanted something much like Gordon and Sandie's Orcas Island home. She and Gordon would agree that he had much more than an advisory role in the design:

Gordon came to town to visit his mom and we took a walk to look at two properties and we agreed on one. I had sketched a design idea for both, and while having dinner that night at Holly Walker's house, I shared the pertinent sketch with Gordon. He added/subtracted from that sketch and slid it back to me— I added to/subtracted from his sketch and passed it back to him. This back-and-forthing went on for about thirty minutes along with discussion, and the house was born.

Since this was my first real house design, having Gordon by my side gave me the confidence I needed. He always gladly picked up the phone just to answer a question or two. Although I

9.4 "Larch": interior. Here the structure can be seen, with neither Conte's braced steel nor Walker's rigid-frame module, although the geometry recalls both. Nice furnishings: An Eames/Herman Miller lounge chair, fiberglass shell rocker with sheepskin throw, and "Eiffel Tower" side chairs surround an antique Franklin stove. Photograph by Andrew van Leeuwen.

9.5 "Larch": the master bedroom. Photograph by Andrew van Leeuwen.

9.6 "Larch," from the falling landscape, touching the earth lightly.
Photograph by Andrew van Leeuwen.

*completed the construction drawings, Gordon took on the details
that allowed that set to come to life. He sketched details for me
and would FedEx them over. Each of those parcels was like opening a present. The way the drawings came as a plan/section/ele-
vation all on one 8½ by 11 sheet was such a lesson in drawing for
me, and a lesson in design.*

Katie's house (2013–14) hovers over its extremely hilly site
on steel posts perched on cast concrete post foundations, echoing
the substructure of Gordon's Orcas house (9.1–9.6). The slope of
Katie's corrugated steel roof is that of the Orcas house and the
Conte house on Lopez. But the similarities are more apparent than
real. Katie hoped to do some of the construction herself, and she
had neither the tools nor the skills to build the steel frames of both
predecessors, so a largely conventional wood frame, with 2 by 8
rafters and 2 by 10 crossties, supports the roof's panels. Other than
plywood sheathing, the wood throughout is larch. Larch is a superb
wood for building, similar to the ubiquitous Douglas fir, workable,
with a close grain, and even fewer knots—and Katie's husband
manages a sawmill that produces dimensioned lumber from old-
growth larch groves. Katie named the house "Larch."

Katie says: "I think Gordon and I both delighted in the fact
that the land I chose was about two blocks from the house he built
during college for his parents. I drive by that house each day, and
I think how it all came full circle for Gordon."

147

10

SCOTT FIFE WAS A STUDENT IN THE DESIGN STUDIO Gordon taught at the University of Idaho in 1970. Scott completed the program, and received a B.Arch. degree, but his passion had turned to art, and those who knew his work agreed that he had an exceptional talent; Gordon thought he was "brilliant." In the early days of Scott's art career, Gordon put him up overnight in the Kirkland studio more than once. Gordon was Best Man at Scott's later marriage to architect Susan Boyle.

In 1975, for the Olson/Walker office, Gordon bought Scott's largest and most notable piece to that date, a near-life-size papier-mâché horse (10.1). It was made from grocery-store bags shaped over a wooden armature, a technique Scott was using at the time for a series of heads of the notable and famous. Gordon liked the horse, and thought it was a significant work of art; he gave it a place in the office, and named it "Horse."

With the passage of time, Scott's reputation grew. In 1982 he was invited to display the sculpture for a year at the Smithsonian. He packed it with appropriate care and sent it on its way. But *Horse* was fragile, and Scott was worried about breakage, prophetically: a leg collapsed in the first week at the Smithsonian, and the neck was broken in the ensuing fall. Scott went to DC for a week to repair the sculpture, strengthening the wooden armature in the process, though he believed it would never again be as it had been. At year's end *Horse* was returned to his place at Olson/Walker.

When Gordon moved to NBBJ in 1986, *Horse* moved with him, loaded into Peter Miller's extensively traveled pickup. Gordon rode with *Horse* in the freight bed, where it slid around—not good. Gordon had to seize some part of the armature to keep the sculpture steady. He grabbed the only exposed member, which happened to be *Horse*'s member. Thus they traveled across Seattle in mid-afternoon.

When Gordon moved Walker Architecture back to Seattle in 1992, *Horse* moved into the newly acquired space. In the first week, Gordon left town to serve on an awards jury. He came back to find *Horse* on his side on the floor, a leg collapsed (again), neck twisted—this amid the din of an alarm system whose turn-off code Gordon hadn't yet memorized. The alarm had called the police. They turned it off, turned on some lights, thought they were looking at a horse murder, almost mirandized Gordon. The next day he bought a horse sling, made some expedient repairs to *Horse*, and suspended him from the office ceiling. There he remained until 2004, when Gordon's daughter Meagan claimed him. At this writing he hangs from her ceiling in his sling, his adventures over.

11 A POETIC ARCHITECTURE

IN HIS EPIGRAPH FOR THIS BOOK Douglas Kelbaugh writes of Gordon's having "charmed an extraordinary number of clients and repeat clients—from California to Seattle to Idaho," and of "the people lucky enough to know this delightful person." Mithun's principals mention Gordon's "personally engaging style." Those on whose projects Gordon works at Mithun say much the same thing, as do his many clients and colleagues, almost without exception. This warmth of personality has been important to the success of Gordon's teaching in design studios at Idaho and Washington, and to his mentoring in many settings. Buildings are another matter. They are expensive things, and while a warm personality can smooth the process of creating one, that is rarely the primary reason for vesting an architect with the responsibility, nor do firms seek personnel, nor universities their planners, for that reason.

Gordon was the lead designer or planner, or the sole architect, for an extraordinary number of architectural projects, several of them at a very large scale. (Gordon is assiduous in giving credit to others involved, but in this he is more gracious than accurate. Unless noted otherwise, the designs featured herein were guided by his hand in all important respects.) Gordon was able to design this extraordinary number of projects because of his unusual way of working. He explores alternatives only in his own mind; outwardly proceeding directly to a single proposal. Evaluating alternatives is a fundamental canon of architectural process, and it is typically done at length, with drawings and verbiage for the record. Yet those who have worked with Gordon usually find that he will have settled on the best of those alternatives almost at the outset, and within a short time will have developed it to a considerable level of resolution. In this manner Gordon has produced designs of quality unusually rapidly, and an extraordinary number of them.

That this is, for him, an effective way of working is evidenced by his experience with the leaders of California's state university system. Having commissioned Gordon to do a modest project at the Irvine campus, they found his work was of such unusual quality that they commissioned him for master plans and individual buildings for Irvine, then for the Davis and San Diego campuses as well. The story is one of many in which clients returned to Gordon for the design of one or more subsequent projects, sometimes over a span of many years. What was it that convinced the California people of his superior abilities, and why did so many other clients, with so many different projects, turn to him, including a major firm that sought him out, and another that was quick to bring him into their upper ranks when the opportunities arose?

A common reason for a first-time client to choose a particular architect lies in the assumption that the architect's past projects indicate the character of future ones: the client likes the way that architect's buildings look or perform, and would like to build something along those lines. But Gordon's buildings are not indicators. Nicholas Court is utterly unlike Hillclimb Court, and neither resembles the Smith townhouses, even though the functions of the three are roughly the same. The Raff, Rogers, and Conte houses are equally unlike. A prospective client could not get, from Gordon's existing work, a clear idea of what that client's building might be like if Gordon were to do it—or to do a second or third design. Therefore it seems unlikely that Gordon's clients came to him, or returned to him, because of the character of his existing buildings. The reason, or reasons, then, must be sought elsewhere.

Before the dominance of modernism, an architect in one of the various earlier eras assumed a finite kit of parts, a formal paradigm from which to construct his design. Iktinos and Kallikrates, in working out the Parthenon; Robert de Luzarches, the first designer of Notre-Dame d'Amiens; Charles Follen McKim, in designing the Morgan Library—each knew the architectural elements he would use to compose, and the ways they should relate to one another.[40]

The advent of the industrial revolution, engendering such structures as the Crystal Palace, the Queensferry Bridge, the Brooklyn Bridge, the Eiffel Tower, the American skyscraper, the great train sheds, inevitably changed the assumptions. The change was given its interpretation for design by Horatio Greenough in the 1840s, and Louis Sullivan in 1896. Each argued that the designer must abandon earlier formal paradigms, and, by implication, not replace them; the form of the artifact must derive only from that artifact's purpose. But Greenough chose easy examples; the sailing ship is an obvious illustration of the point. And in his "form ever follows function," Sullivan had in mind a broad interpretation; he saw the rose as an example.

With the triumph of modernism in the twentieth century, the phrase became a commonplace canon. But as it relates to the architect's task, it seriously misleads. Most functions that architecture serves can be happily clad in any number of formal possibilities. This has left the modern architect with a truly formidable task—for, rejecting any kit of parts whatsoever, that architect, if he obeys the mandate, must devise each form with frighteningly little guidance —none at all, really. Many a college campus and metropolitan street can testify that the process hasn't always yielded success.

Some architects have devised their own kit of parts, and their work is recognizable for having done so: Mies is a handy example; the late work of Edward Stone is an extreme one; Wright devised at least three kits. Gordon, however, seems always to take the difficult path: he begins every project from scratch, and so each is unlike any of its predecessors in any obvious way. Although he is unusual in this, he is far from alone: as one of many other examples, Eero Saarinen's MIT chapel, Dulles International Airport, and TWA Flight Center differ in utterly fundamental ways; no like appearances there.

But although Gordon's buildings differ from one another in significant and evident ways, his designs have two characteristics in common: they are all rigorously ordered, and they are all extremely complex. This is true of Doug and Kathie Raff's house with its space-articulating wing walls, and their house on Whidbey, the Rogers design with its paired beams, the Conte house with its insistent spine, the streetscape of the Smith town houses. Gordon is quite conscious of this; he will state plainly that his first objective

in designing is to discover or devise an appropriate order, then to develop within it a richness of complexities. In this way he creates an architecture of order and complexity, or complex order. At this level of abstraction Gordon's work has common ground with music, or dance, or poetry—complexly ordered phenomena all. Thus it is possible to speak of his architecture as poetic.

As a vestige of his student and teaching days, Gordon gives architectural examples a report-card grade, sometimes declared, more often kept to himself in a kind of internal monolog. He is no fan of grade inflation: friend Peter Miller, whose wife, Colleen, has worked with Gordon for some years, says: "Everyone wants to work for Gordon, but no one wants to be graded by him." Asked what work makes his honors list, he immediately cites Wright's Unity Temple, then, after a pause, "those Gothic cathedrals—Civita"— a longer pause—"Aalto's Villa Mairea, maybe the Saarinens' Cranbrook, Kahn's Museum of British Art, Schindler's Newport Beach house, La Maison de Verre…" After a slow start, it turns out to be quite a long list.

But those examples are by others. What of his own work? This book has included very few comments by Gordon about his own accomplishments, because he says very little about them, and nothing at all in the way of extravagant praise. His utter absence of self-congratulation is an outward manifestation of a bone-marrow-deep inner modesty. He might concede, reluctantly, after trying to change the subject a few times, that the Raff house deserves an A-minus. He likes the Smith town houses, the Nicholas apartments, his own early apartment at Pike and Virginia—he thinks they are in the B to B-plus range. And when it is put to him that designing as he does—rapid apprehension yielding a poetic architecture, over the broadest spectrum of architectural challenges—and that this remarkable ability is rare, possibly unique, Gordon will only say: "When I chose architecture as my life's work, I wanted to be an above-average architect. And I think I've made it; I think I'm an above-average architect."

12 COGNATE THOUGHTS

JEFFREY MURDOCK

GORDON'S MANY REPEAT CLIENTS ARE TESTAMENT to his ability to design a building that meets their prima facie needs; he also usually becomes a friend. The clients may have appreciated taking part in the design process as well as the product. But their satisfaction also seems to have come from something more—we recall Kathie Raff's belief that the house brought them to "a category of awareness that influenced almost everything that followed" in their lives, though she did not describe what that something more might be. Architects and architectural theorists, moreover, have a challenging time defining what is meant by "quality" in architecture, why it is that the phrase "a work of architecture" is understood to mean something other than "a building."

This book has emphasized complex order as one measure, likening it to music, dance, poetry. Colin St John Wilson offers a complementary view. He describes the architectural masterpiece as a work that addresses the "polar modes." By this he means that to be emotionally meaningful to the human user, to touch the soul, the building must do more than be structurally sound and satisfy the client's pragmatic needs. Vitruvius would agree, of course: firmness and commodity are not enough. St John Wilson argues that architectural poetry lies in drawing from the full range of human experience and memory, that this will entail polar extremes of experience: comfort will accompany peril; interior and exterior will merge; the ambience will be both welcoming and defensive. An architecture that can embody these characteristics is, to St John Wilson, a masterpiece.

We have discussed how Gordon's apartment in the Pike and Virginia building represents a complex counterpoint to the building's universal sense of order. Standing in the living room,

one does not have an understanding of the limits of the modest space. At the southwest corner of the apartment, the location of the dining room, the ceiling rises upward, out of view, as the steel-frame window system angles unexpectedly to the concrete wall. One does not have a sense of where the dining room ends and the exterior world begins. Along the back of the apartment, hunkered against a subterranean parking garage, a wall of illuminated glass block creates a sense of daylight shining into the space, where no daylight exists. This sense of wonderment is characteristic of the masterpiece.

There are experiences in Gordon's designs that engage a human need for risk and reassurance; the elevated bridges in his Kirkland house conveyed the thrill of a backyard tree house. The balcony of the Raff house, that overlooks the two-story dining space, draws one to the edge of an internal precipice; the vicarious danger of falling is thrilling, and thrill is a paradoxical word in its inclusion of both fear and pleasure. In every case, however, the design provides the safe, solid, comforting counterpoint, what St John Wilson would call an all-embracing, sheltering feeling of protection.

Gordon's buildings have a timeless quality; they never exhibit the architectural fashion of a specific period. The Raff house might have been designed last year, or—almost—carved from stone in some prehistoric settlement. In each of his houses, there is an expression of joy; the buildings convey the intentions of a boy living a Wild West dream: fishing on a Cascade mountain lake; repairing an old lodge in an abandoned town; falling in love; fabricating wooden light fixtures; and laying concrete blocks, the next and the next and the next, until imagination becomes built form.

NOTES

INTRODUCTION

1. Appleton spoke at the University of Washington in 1978, and I was immediately interested in his ideas, from which came *The Wright Space: Pattern and Meaning in Frank Lloyd Wright's Houses* (Seattle: University of Washington Press, 1991), and *Origins of Architectural Pleasure* (Berkeley: University of California Press, 1999). Appleton was the John Danz Lecturer at Washington in 1991.

2. See note 1.

3. For two fireplaces and a revolving bed, in Lovett's 1994 additions to the villa for Charles Simonyi, in Medina, on the eastern shore of Lake Washington. Both bed and fireplaces are illustrated in Grant Hildebrand and T. William Booth, *A Thriving Modernism* (Seattle: University of Washington Press, 2004), p. 104.

1 A HOUSE FOR THE RAFFS

4. Letter from Katherine Raff to the author, July 2017.

5. This and similar quotations throughout the book are from conversations between Gordon and the author from June 2017 through August 2018. Sources of quotations not from those conversations will be identified as they occur.

6. *Sunset*, October 1971, p. 79.

2 GORDON'S EARLY YEARS

7. One, caught by Gordon in his college years and published in *Field and Stream*, weighed 28 pounds, a record for that year.

8. This would include Paul Rudolph, Philip Johnson, Gordon Bunshaft of Skidmore, Owings, and Merrill, Edward Stone, Minoru Yamasaki, even Eero Saarinen, who had trained with his father, Eliel, at the decidedly un-Miesian Cranbrook Academy.

9. By 1960 several other books about Wright had appeared, notably Wright's own *Testament* of 1957, and his *Autobiography* could be had in both the 1932 and 1942 editions, although neither was illustrated. The serial *Architectural Forum* dedicated its entire issues of January 1938, January 1948, and June 1959 to Wright's work. Neither these publications, nor any other at that time, was more extensive in its inclusions and their discussion than Hitchcock's book.

10. Gordon's siblings were "ski instructors, gentleman ranchers, general handymen." Gordon was the only one of the four to pursue a "normal (more or less) life pattern."

11. One can still be amazed by the height of Amiens, but no one can again experience Gordon's epiphany at Chartres. Because of a belief that it was so originally, restorationists have painted the entire interior of that greatest of cathedrals a light tan, thus washing out the contrast of the dark stone walls with the famous brilliant glass. With that, the experience that for centuries has been universally agreed to have been one of the great achievements of Western Civilization is gone. This has also been done at Notre-Dame de Paris, Saint-Denis, and elsewhere. Ruskin's 1849 essay "Lamp of Memory" spoke to the value of the time dimension in the architectural experience. That is now irreversibly gone at those sites. Will the cupped steps of the chapter house stair at Wells some day be replaced by new ones that are straight and true, since that's how they were "originally"?

12. In one of the fields the farmer saw them, called them over, told them the corn was for animals, not humans.

13. These were the days when one got a pretty good meal on a lengthy flight, usually a nice little menu with choice of entrée, at no charge, and so Bobbie and Gordon would soon be fed.

14. Among them: William Booth, Dave Fukui, Ron Murphy, Jim Olson, Jerry Stickney, George Suyama, and Gordon.

15. This quote is from her obituary in the *Seattle Times*, Friday, October 13, 2000. Jean's career included interiors for the governor's mansion in Olympia, Canlis restaurant with architect Roland Terry, and the Sunset Club with artist Leo Adams. In 1995 the Bellevue Art Museum curated a retrospective of her career.

3 OLSON/WALKER 1970–78

16. In 1977 Bagley Wright would retain Arthur Erickson to design a residence that was equally a family dwelling and a gallery for art.

17. Jim Olson designed a retreat for himself and his family at Longbranch that is one of the finest examples of what I have called the Puget Sound School.

18. Eberharter and Gaunt; Roy Gaunt was the partner associated with the job.

19. Gordon notes that they were from Montana; "they had guts."

20. In admitting natural light into a space, the upper part of a window contributes far more than the lower portions; the higher the window the better. Thus the second-floor glazing in this case vastly increases the illumination of the spaces within.

4 OLSON/WALKER 1978–85

21. In that same year Johnson perused a compilation of projects by the Puget Sound School. He said, with some awe, that this body of work was "magnificent," and wondered why he had never encountered any of it before.

22. The building was designed as a poured-in-place concrete flat slab

structure. Columns in a flat-slab design must have broad capitals, of one shape or another, to provide a generous bearing area. The capitals at the 1904 site are, conceptually, octagonal in plan, of which only a little less than half is seen because of the walls along the structural centerlines.

23. Bebb was in Seattle to supervise construction of Sullivan's design for the Seattle Opera House. The firm was still Adler and Sullivan at that time. The project was killed by the depression of '93, but Bebb stayed in Seattle for the remainder of his life, becoming a partner in the major firm of Bebb and Gould.

5   GORDON, 1985–90

24. Minoru Yamasaki was one of the jurors for Astra's final presentation for the B.Arch. degree from the University of Washington in 1953. After graduation she worked for Paul Hayden Kirk for about a year, then was admitted to MIT, obtaining a M.Arch. degree in 1955. She then entered Yamasaki's office. She was a lead designer, and did many of the presentation drawings, in the era in which the firm acquired an abundance of awards and international recognition. Her excellence in teaching was recognized by her receipt, in 1979, of the UW's Distinguished Teaching Award, its highest teaching accolade.

25. Won by Paul Thiry, whose design, its hovering white roof striking as

seen from the street, is one of his most graceful achievements.

6   WALKER ARCHITECTURE

26. Wikipedia: Castilleja School is an independent 6–12 school for girls, in Palo Alto. Castilleja is the only such nonsectarian private school in the Bay Area.

27. Among other things Frank Lloyd Wright said about the American Institute of Architects, he remarked that it really ought to be the American Institute of Architecture.

28. Of Paul Thiry it should be added that among other accomplishments, he was architect for the Washington State Pavilion at the Exposition. Now known as the Key Arena, the pavilion was a fascinatingly inventive suspension structure. Four panels used a hyperbolic paraboloid configuration to obtain from the cables a suspension structural capability. The cables were tied to four huge concrete beams, supported in turn by four great concrete buttresses of considerable sculptural elegance. The building has been remodeled structurally, and is no longer a suspension structure; the hyperbolic paraboloid panels are now simpler faux-suspension concrete shells.

29. The Olmsted plan for the campus was one of the firm's few flawed designs, a rigid scheme that failed to exhibit any convincing idea. Fortunately the plan was overtaken by

events: the A-Y-P Exposition of 1909 determined much of the successful Bebb and Gould plan of 1915, still evident. See also Norman J. Johnston, *University of Washington: The Campus Guide*, Princeton University Press, 2001, pp. 4–5.

30. Colleen and Colin did many of the contract drawings.

31. See Grant Hildebrand and T. William Booth, *A Thriving Modernism: The Houses of Wendell Lovett and Arne Bystrom,* Seattle, University of Washington Press, 2004, pp. 37–41

32. She came around, to become an equally dedicated Seattlite. See *ARCADE* online website.

33. With Colleen Miller as project architect.

34. The thicknesses of architectural materials throw simple dimensions to the winds. In this case, the walls are 16 feet apart measured from center to center of studs, but the distance between inner faces is then about 15 feet 9½ inches, outer faces about 16 feet 4¼ inches, depending on stud width and inner and outer cladding. Hence "nominal" for the 16 feet in this sentence, and elsewhere.

35. Colin drafted most of the contract drawings; Rachel King supervised construction and assisted with installation of landscape features.

36. The house was featured, with seven photographs, in *Seattle Homes and Lifestyles* for August 2002, pp. 44–49.

7   GORDON AT MITHUN

37. Bert Gregory, sometime CEO of Mithun, participated in seminars and conferences in what Steven Kellert called Biophilia; see Heerwagen, Mador, and Kellert, *Biophilic Design*, New York, Wiley, 2008.

8   A PREFAB ON ORCAS ISLAND

38. See Herbert, Gilbert, *The Dream of the Factory-Made House, Walter Gropius and Konrad Wachsmann*, Cambridge, MA: MIT, 1984.

9   TEACHER AND MENTOR

39. The studios of 1992 and 1998 were cotaught with the author.

11   A POETIC ARCHITECTURE

40. McKim, Mead, and White, and their colleagues working in the Shingle Style, however, created an exquisite expression of the unique American balloon-frame construction system; the Goelet house, the Newport Casino, now Tennis Hall of Fame, Manchester-by-the-Sea, are examples. This was a case of form following construction system rather than function, but it is an interesting contemporaneous cousin to Sullivan's canon.

TIMELINE

1962   1963   1964   1965   1966   1967   1968   1969

1962

Bachelor of Architecture

Worked for Ralph Decker,
Seattle, WA

1963-1965

Worked with Ralph Anderson,
Seattle, WA

Smith residence, Ellensburg, WA

1965-1966

*Designed and built my first house
for my family in Champagne Point,
Kirkland, WA*

*Raff #1 residence on Queen Anne,
Seattle, WA, designed and built*

*Spec townhouse, Mount Baker, Seattle,
WA, codesigned with Jim Olson, and
built by GW*

1968-1970

*Seattle, WA, residences: Waddington,
Mercer Island; Rogers #1, Juanita Beach;
Lowery #1, Denny Blaine*

Shared Seattle office space with
Jim Olson

*Friday Harbor residence, San Juan
Island, WA*

1970 1971 1972 1973 1974 1975 1976 1977

1970-1972

Taught full-time at University of
Idaho, Moscow

*Designed, built, and was part owner of
the Bakery Restaurant, Pioneer Square
(now Grand Central Bakery)*

*WA residences: Kundstater
(design+build), Evergreen Point; Hofer,
Yakima*

Cofounded Olson/Walker
(1970-1985) with Jim Olson

1974-1976

Taught design studio at University of
Washington

Green Lake sailing and boating facility

Maynard Building, Pioneer Square

Miscellaneous Pioneer Square remodels

Bellevue, WA, residences: Coons; Potter

*The Good Shepherd Center (original
home of Pacific Northwest Ballet)*

1972-1974

*Community parks: Lake City
and Kenmore, WA*

Pioneer Square remodels

Tonn residence, Spokane, WA

*Seattle, WA, residences: Sandberg,
Livengood, Bates*

1976-1978

*Smith Town Houses (multifamily),
Seattle, WA*

Taught design studio at University of
Washington

*Walker residence addition, Champagne
Point, Kirkland, WA*

Served on Pioneer Square Historic
Preservation Board

1978   1979   1980   1981   1982   1983   1984   1985

1980-1982

Pike and Virginia, Pike Place Market, Seattle, WA—owner, architect, developer, partnership with Jim Olson, designed and built personal unit

Lowry #2, Lake Sammamish, WA

1904 restaurant, Seattle, WA, part owner

Waterfront Reprographics, part owner

1984-1986

Ongoing commercial work

Applied Physics Lab, University of Washington

Merrill Place, in collaboration with NBBJ

Future development planning for Western Avenue, Seattle, WA— coordinated the design efforts of two major developers and their architects

Waterfront Place, Portland, OR, with Bumgardner Architects

Left Olson/Walker

1982-1983

Cofounded the Gang of Five

Hillclimb Court, Seattle, WA—designed and built personal unit

Tacoma, WA: Financial Center; Tacoma Center; Cornerstone Building and Market off Broadway

Broadway Development master plan, Tacoma, WA

Seattle Center master plan for the City of Seattle, with Grant Jones and David Hancocks

Mark Tobey Pub, Seattle, WA, part owner

1978-1980

Boyce residence, Whidbey Island, WA

160

1986   1987   1988   1989   1990   1991   1992   1993

1988–1990

NBBJ office relocation to the Hallidie Building in San Francisco, CA

Miscellaneous University of California projects: two research buildings (UC Davis), classroom and student services building (UC San Diego), campus conceptual plans, programs and mini master plans on other campuses

Warren Thoits Building, Palo Alto, CA

Castilleja School master plan, Palo Alto, CA

1992–1994

Moved back to Seattle

Taught design studio at University of Washington

Miscellaneous remodels

University of Idaho, Moscow, conceptual design and visualization planning for the future buildout of the campus master plan, completed with RHAA Landscape Architects

1986–1988

Joined NBBJ, Seattle

Taught design studio at University of Washington with Grant Hildebrand

Designed two unbuilt towers at Third and University for Canadian Pacific Rail and Land Development Division

Carpenter Hall, Washington State University, Pullman

University of California Davis, master plan

Raff residence #2, Whidbey Island, WA

Pacific Northwest Ballet/Phelps Center, with NBBJ

Moved to San Francisco's NBBJ office

1990–1992

Left NBBJ

Started Walker Architecture in San Francisco, CA

University of Idaho, Moscow, master plan with RHAA Landscape Architects, Mill Valley, CA

Two California residences and miscellaneous remodels

Ross residence, Seattle, WA

Princeton Bio Center conceptual master plan, Princeton, NJ

1994 1995 1996 1997 1998 1999 2000 2001

1998–2000

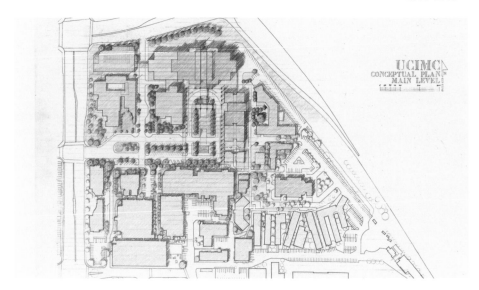

Jensen/Meleliot residence, Seattle, WA

Conte residence #1, Seattle, WA

Pacific Northwest Ballet, Francia Russell Center #1, Bellevue, WA

Miscellaneous remodels

UC Irvine medical school master plan and concept for new hospital, with NBBJ

Hewitt Hall, student recreation center with Carrier Johnson, UC Irvine, CA

1994–1996

Rogers residence #2, Lopez Island, WA

Ongoing concept planning and student commons for University of Idaho, Moscow

Design Consultant with YGH, Portland — Albertson Building, University of Idaho, Moscow

University of Idaho: assisted with architectural designs for new student commons, teaching and learning center, student housing, administration buildings, and the Lionel Hampton School of Music

Miscellaneous remodels

2000–2002

Washington residences: Williams, Seattle; Conte #2, Lopez Island; Stowell/Russell, Whidbey Island

Nicholas Court (multifamily), Seattle, WA, with son Colin Walker

Delaurenti Delicatessen remodel, Pike Place Market, Seattle, WA

Closed Walker Architecture at age 65

Taught design studio at University of Washington

2002   2003   2004   2005   2006   2018

2002–2017

Joined Mithun as consulting principal

Portland projects, Block 136

Seattle mixed-use projects

Pacific Northwest Ballet, Francia Russell Center #2, Bellevue, WA, with Mithun

Coeur d'Alene Resort and Casino, Coeur d'Alene, ID

Russell/Stowell residence, Whidbey Island, WA

2006–2018

Pope/Walker residence, Orcas Island, WA

Miscellaneous remodels on Orcas and San Juan Islands

Cox residence, Sandpoint, ID—assisted designer and home-owner, Katie Cox

Youngren residence, Orcas Island, WA

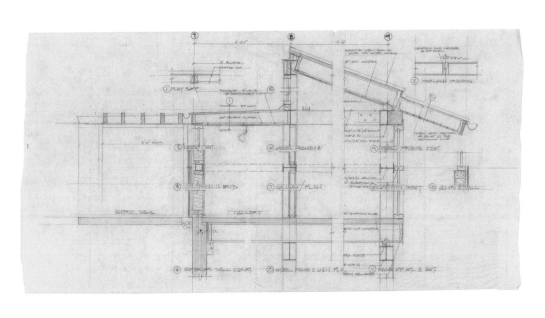

DRAWINGS

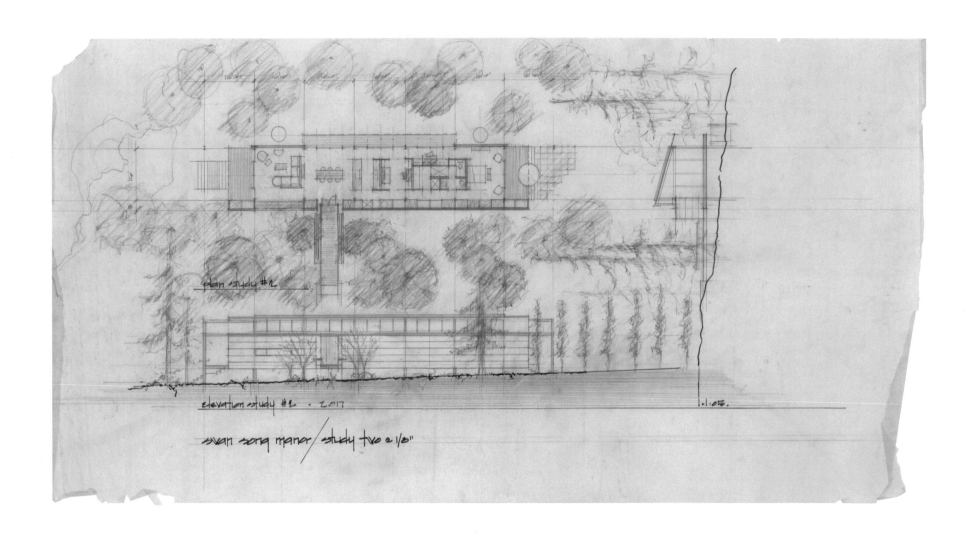

plan study #2

elevation study #2 · 2017

swan song manor / study two @ 1/8"

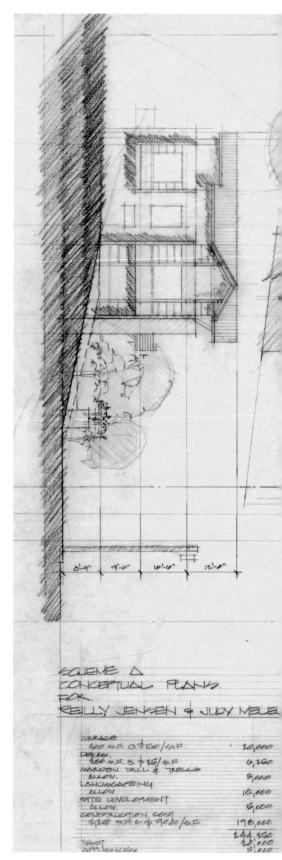

SCHEME A
CONCEPTUAL PLANS
FOR
REILLY JENSEN & JUDY MELE

Oil painting made in class, 1962.

Early schematic drawing of the
Jensen Meleliot residence, Seattle,
WA, 2000.

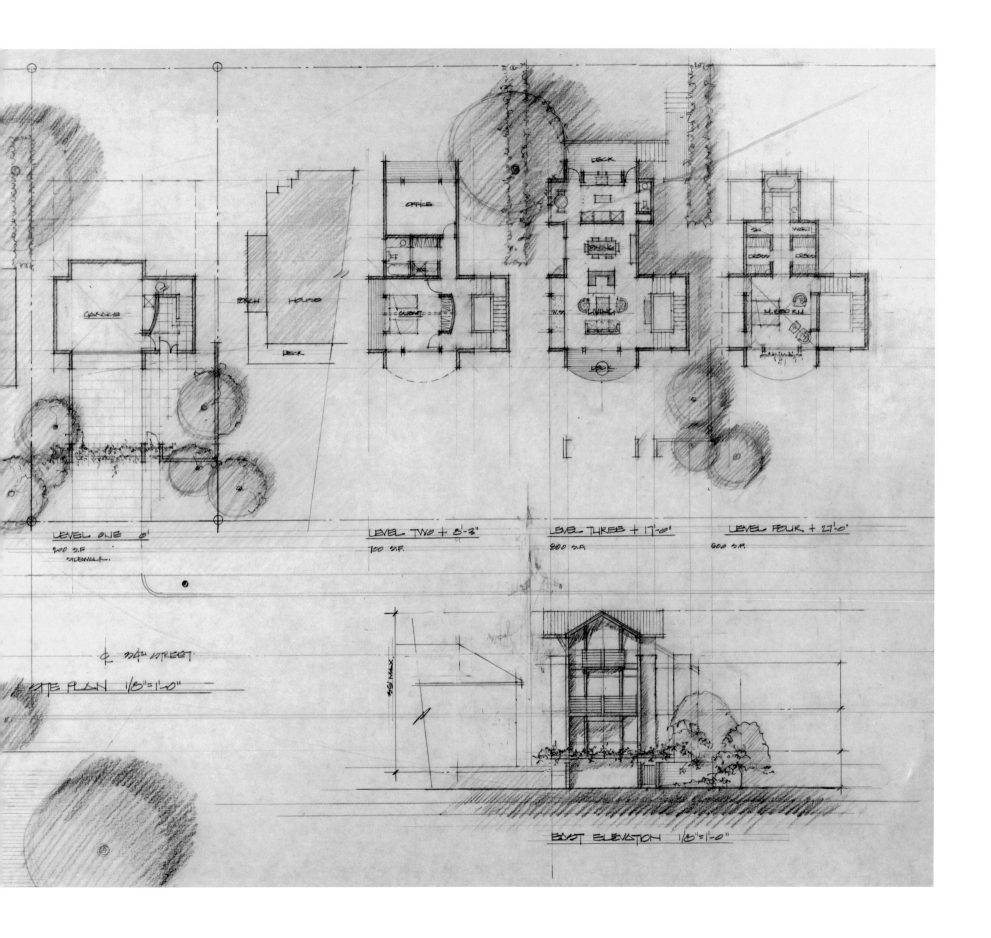

LEVEL ONE   0'

200 S.F.
SIDEWALK.

LEVEL TWO + 8'-3"

700 S.F.

LEVEL THREE + 17'-0"

800 S.F.

LEVEL FOUR + 27'-0"

500 S.F.

GARAGE

PORCH   HOUSE

DECK

OFFICE

GUEST

OFFICE

DECK

DINING

W.S.   LIVING

DECK

SH.   W.C.

CLOS.   CLOS.

M. BED RM.

₵ 34ᵗʰ STREET

SITE PLAN 1/8"=1'-0"

35' MAX.

EAST ELEVATION 1/8"=1'-0"

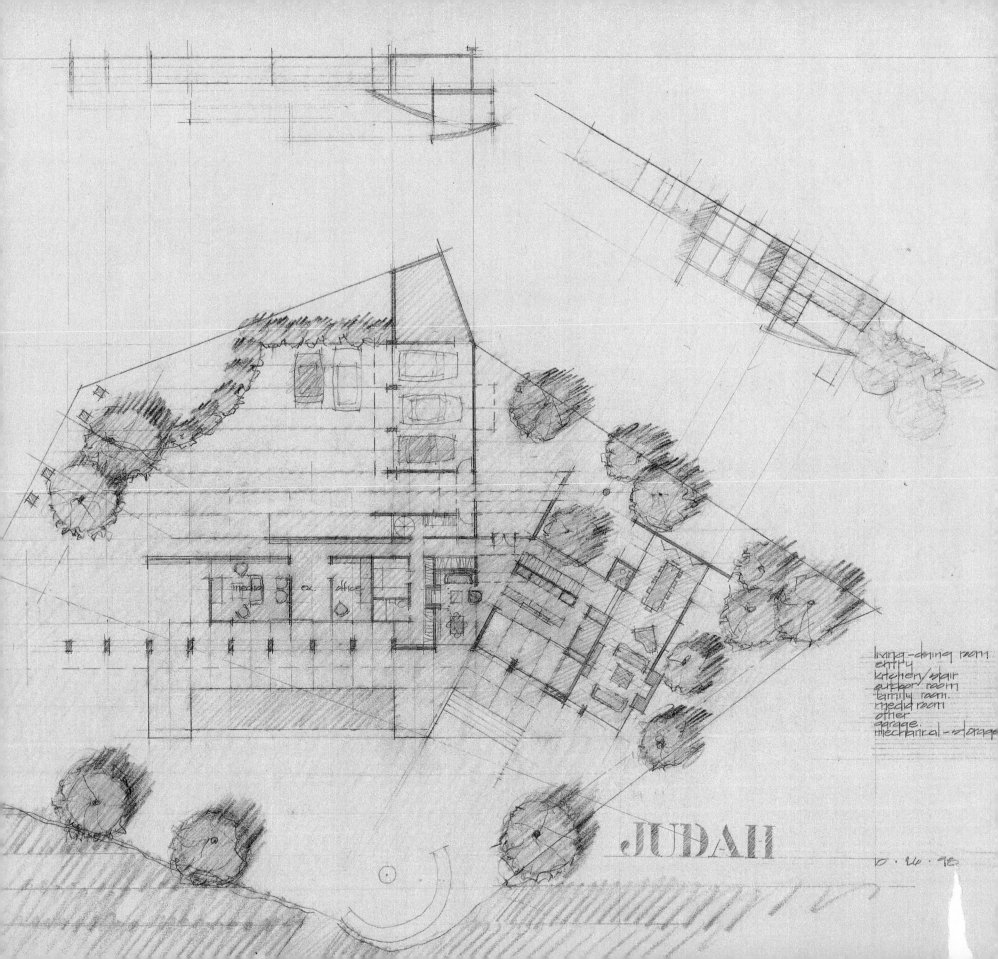

living-dining room
entry
kitchen/stair
outdoor room
family room
media room
other
garage
mechanical-storage

media   ex.   office

JUDAH

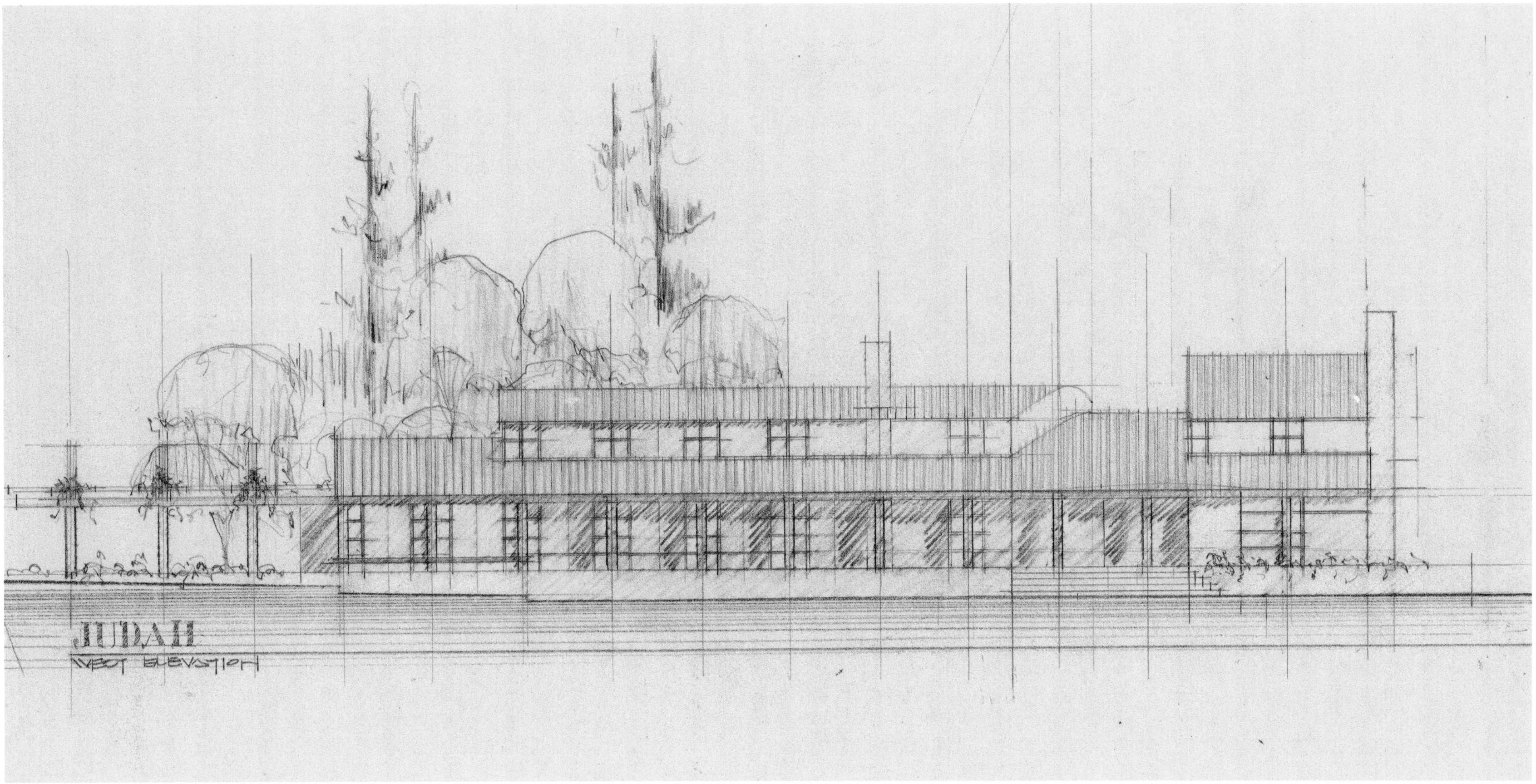
JUDAH
WEST ELEVATION

Mercer Island, WA, residence, 2001.

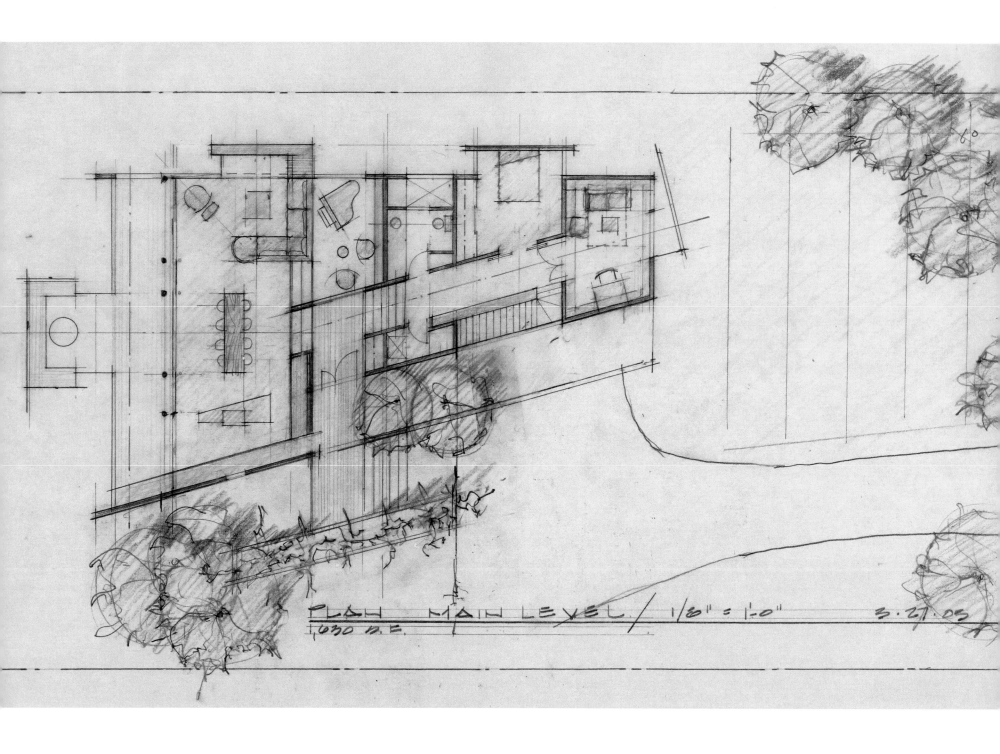

PLAN MAIN LEVEL / 1/8" = 1'-0" 3.27.03
630 A.E.

Conceptual plan and schematic elevation (facing page) for the Stowell-Russell Whidbey Island, WA, residence, 2004.

Oil painting made in class, 1962.

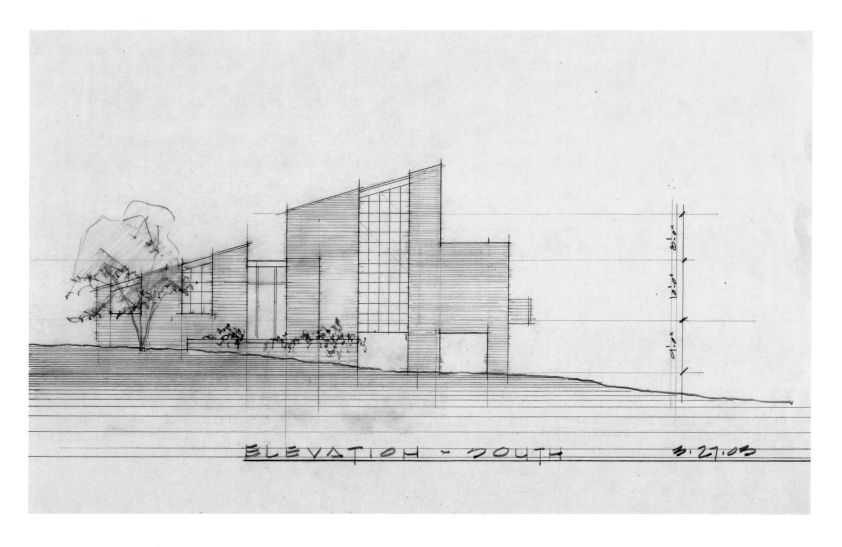

ELEVATION ~ SOUTH   3.27.03

PLAN/UPPER LEVEL

PLAN/MAIN LEVEL

NORTH PROPERTY LINE

GARDEN

ORCHARD

WASH

PUMP

PARKING

SOUTH PROPERTY LINE

GREAT

MBR

DINING

VITALS.

MAIN LEVEL
  750 S.F @ 150/SF   112,500
TERRACE
  500 S.F @ 50/SF   25,000
PORCH
  200 S.F @ 60/SF   12,000
WASH & PUMP HOUSE
  200 S.F @ 80/SF   16,000
UPPER LEVEL
  375 S.F @ 130/SF   48,750
GARDEN & LANDSCAPE
  ALLOW   15,000

TTL $ 229,250
W.S.S.T.   18,500

rogers-lopez

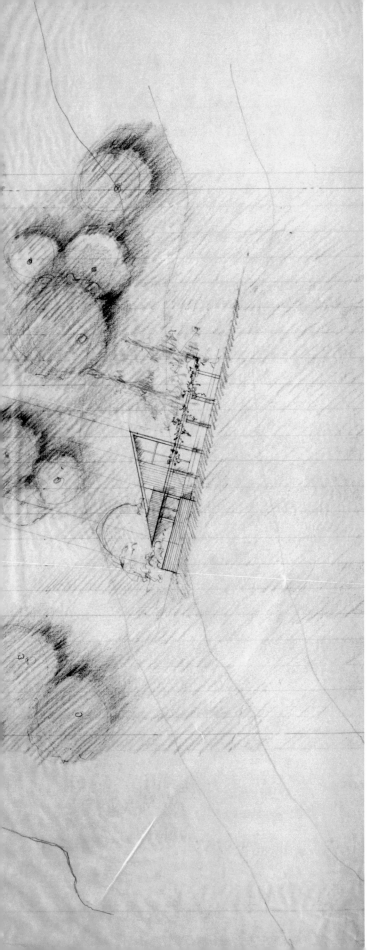

First schematic design for the Rogers
Lopez Island, WA, cabin, 1998.   173

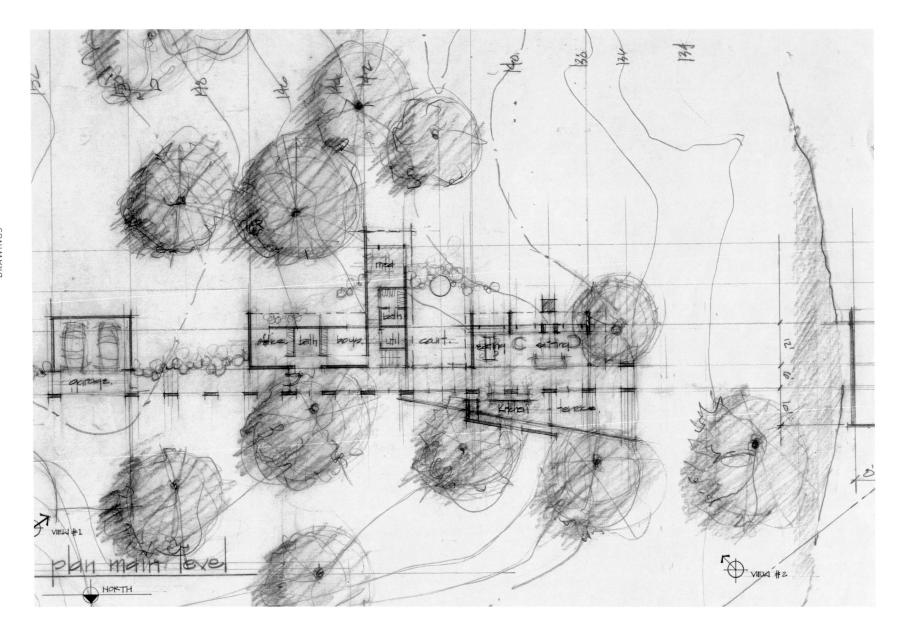

VIEW #1

plan main level

NORTH

VIEW #2

Early schematic design of the Conte
174   Lopez Island, WA, cabin, 2000.

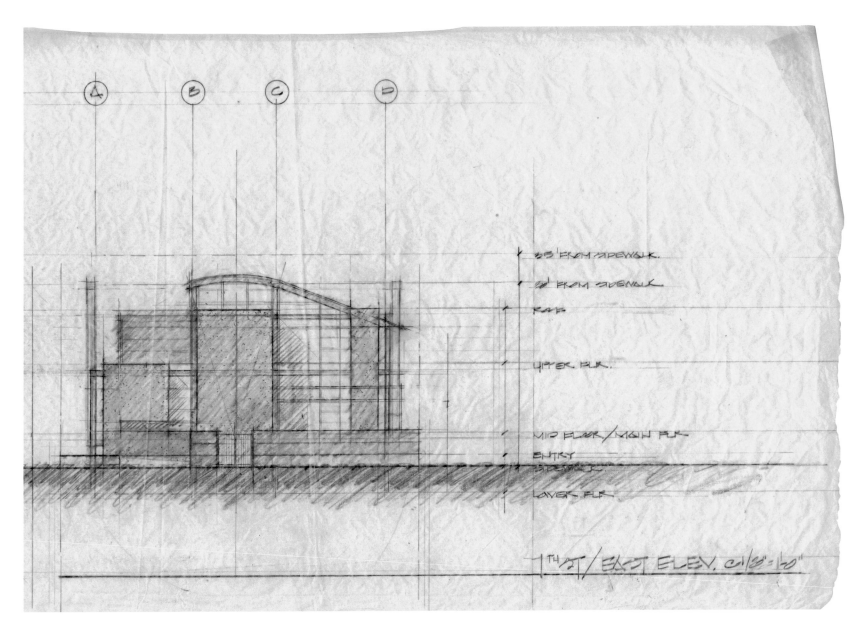

35' FROM SIDEWALK.
30' FROM SIDEWALK
ROOF
UPPER FLR.
MID FLOOR/MAIN FLR
ENTRY
SIDEWALK
LOWER FLR

7TH ST / EAST ELEV. c1/8"=1'0"

Early schematic design of the
Williams residence, 2001.

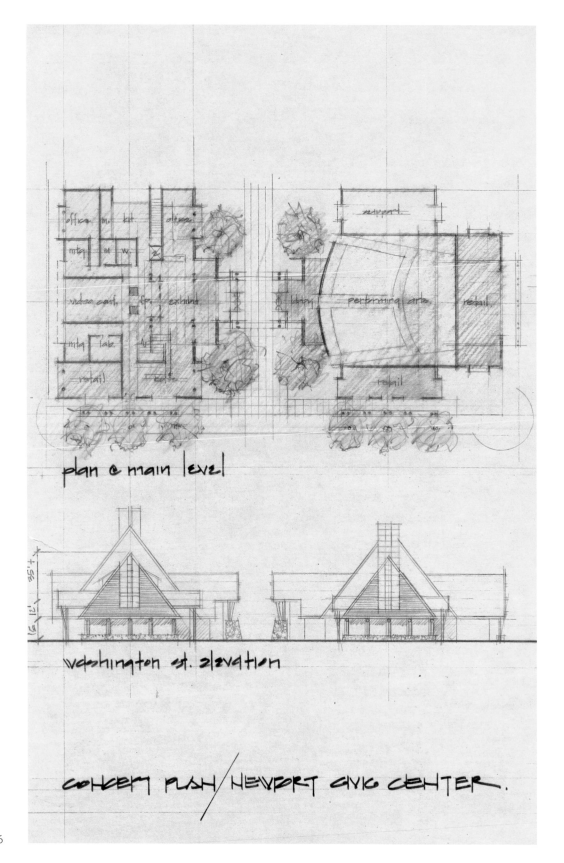

plan @ main level

washington st. elevation

concept plan / newport civic center.

A design proposal for a small, log-timber community and performing arts center in Newport, WA, 2000 (unbuilt).

Conceptual plan and building documents for the Crosby studio, Orcas Island, WA, 2017.

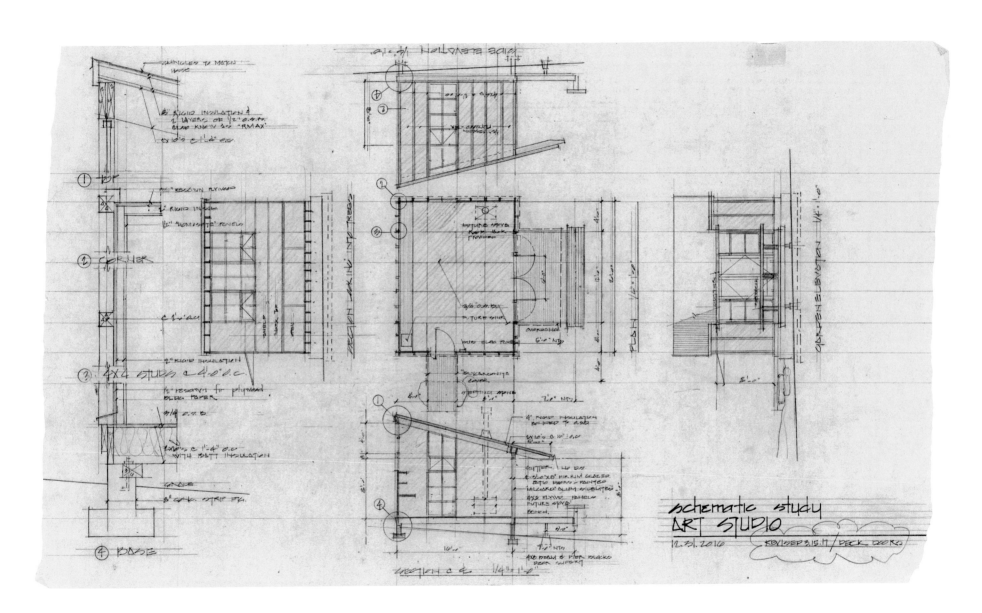

schematic study
ART STUDIO
12.31.2016   REVISED 3.15.17 / DECK DOORS

Schematic drawing of the Youngren
Orcas Island, WA, residence, under
178 construction, 2019.

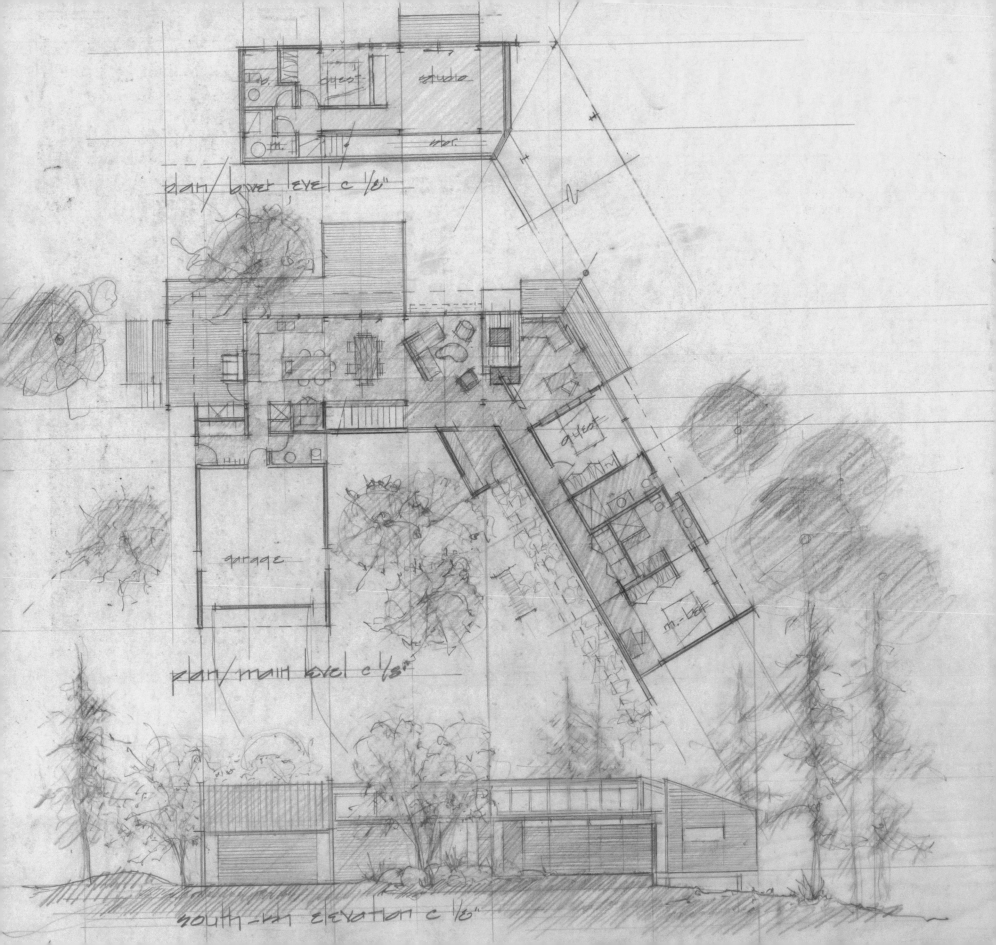

plan/ lower level c 1/8"

guest   studio

stor.

plan/ main level c 1/8"

garage

guest

m. bd.

south-west elevation c 1/8"

INDEX

Italicized page numbers indicate illustrations.

Aalto, Alvar, *102*, 152
Aluminum Company of America (ALCOA), 129
American Institute of Architects (AIA): AIA-Sunset Magazine Western Home Awards Citation (1971–1972), 28; Gordon and, 36, 76, 82, 141; Mithun in College of Fellows, 115; National Honor Award (1976), 54; Seattle Honor Awards (1979, 1983), 59
Anderson, Ralph, 11, 14, *14*, 17, 28, 40–43, 47, 51
Appleton, Jay, 11, 156n1
Architectural Digest, 138

Bain, William, Jr., 78
Bebb and Gould, 73, 157n23, 157n29
Bebb and Mendel, *72*, 73
Bellevue, Washington: Bellevue Clinic, *14*; Francia Russell Center, 106–8, *109*, *123*, 124
Birkerts, Gunnar, 75, 76
Bo, Jorgen, 40
Booth, T. William, 43, 79, 156n14
Boyle, Susan, 149

Callison Architects, 88
Calvin, Dan, 28, 43
Chareau, Pierre, 59
Chartres cathedral, 156n11
Chervenak, Robert, *41*, 43
Chicago: Keck and Keck's work in, 47; Wright's works in, 36
Civita di Bagnoregio, 75, 76, 152
complex order: 11, 28, 54, 67, 79, *80*, 102, 152

Conte, Michael, 93, 102–6
Conte house (Lopez Island): bedrooms, *104*, 106, *108*; comparisons with, *144–45*, 147, 151; design plan of, 102, *105*, 106, 152; exterior and colonnade, 102, *104–5*, 106; kitchen and dining space, *104*, 106, *106*; living space, *104*, 106, *106*, *108*
Cool, Gale, 59
Cornerstone Development Company, 67, *68–71*, 72
Cox, Katie Egland, *142*, 144–47

Davis (later Basetti), Gwenyth, 52
Decker, Ralph, 39

Fife, Scott, 52, 149; *Horse*, 149, *149*
Fisher, Elmer, 73
Fukui, David, 28, 43, 156n14
Fuller, Buckminster, 129

Gaudí, Antonio, 40
Goldberg, Dave, 8, 115
Gold Rush, 127–29
Green Lake Sailing and Boating Facility, *63–63*, *64–65*
Gregory, Bert, 115, 157n37
Gropius, Walter, 127, 129

Hagen, Emily, 123
Halladie Building, 78–79, *79*
Hampton, Lionel, 88
Hewitt, David, 28, 73
Hillclimb Court, *67–72*, 75, 76, 151
Hitchcock, Henry-Russell, 35, 36, 156n9

Hook, Bill, 8, *17*, *18*, *42*, *43*, *44*, *48*, *49*, *50*, *52*, *56*, *77*, *78*, *83*, *95*, *100*
Hopkins, Gerard Manley, 28
Horse, 149, *149*
HOWDI (1985), 73, *73*

Isley, Bill, 73

Jacobson, Arne, 40
James, Pat, 75–76
Jensen, Bob: *Stroke* (sculpture), 63, 65
Johnson, Philip, 35, 64, 156n8, 156n21
Jongeward, Jean, 11, 43, 51, 156n15

Kahn, Louis: 36–37, Museum of British Art, 152; talk in DC, 36; Trenton bath houses, 14
Keck and Keck, 47
Kelbaugh, Douglas, 4, 151
King, Rachel, 93, 108, 142–44, 157n35
Kirk, Paul Hayden, 11, 14, 35, *35*, 39, *41*, 43, 77, *77*, 85
Kirkland, Washington: "House in the Trees"; "Children's House," *42*, 43, 155; studio, 43, 44
Koch, Carl, 129
Kunstadler house, 47–48, *50–51*

"Larch", 140–47
Lewerentz, Sigurd, 40
LMN Architects, 78
Longfellow, Henry Wadsworth, 28
Lopez Island. *See* Conte house; Rogers house

Lovett, Wendell, 11, 90, 156n3
Luzarches, Robert de, 151

Madison, Wisconsin: Pew house, 37, *37*
Maison de Verre, La, 59
Marathon Towers, 77–78, *78*
Maynard, David Swinson "Doc," 52
McKim, Charles Follen, 151
McKim, Mead, and White, 157n40
Mercer Island, Washington: City Hall, 75; Waddington house, 47, *48–49*
Meleliot house, 90, *90*
Merrill Place, *72*, 73
Mies van der Rohe, Ludwig, 35, *35*, 40, 152
Miller, Colleen, 79–80, *82*, 88, 108, 142, 144, 152, 157n30, 157n33
Miller, Peter, 9, 11, 76, 79–80, *82*, 149, 152
Mithun, Omer, 115, 116
Mithun, 115–25; design process at, 119; Gordon as Consulting Principal at, 11, 106, *114*, 115–24, *116–17*, 141–42, 151; San Francisco office of, 115; Seattle office of, 115, *116–17*, 122
Morris, Abbie and Scott, 43
Mount Baker house, 43, 45
Murcutt, Glenn, 85, 129
Murdock, Jeffrey, 8

NBBJ (Naramore, Bain, Brady, & Johanson), 11; 73; 76–78; 80–82; 88; 115
Nicholas Court, 92–97, 93, 102, 151

1904 Restaurant, 64–67, *66–67*, 69
Nordstrom, Illsley, 64

Olmsted, John Charles, 86
Olson, Jim, 13, 28, 43–45, 47, *48–51*, *58*, 59, 73, 156n14, 156n17. *See also* Olson/Walker
Olson/Sundberg, 73, 75
Olson/Walker, 11, 47–73, 76; change to Olson/Sundberg, 73, 75; collaboration with NBBJ, 73; Gordon's resignation from, 73; at Fix-Madore building, 73; office at Pike and Virginia Building (1974–75), *58*, 58–59; weekly "crit" sessions, 51–52; work from Schell and Youngren, 67, *178*. *See also specific projects or locations*
Orcas Island, Moran State Park picnic shelter, 88, *128*
Orcas Island home, 125, 127–38, *128*; bedroom and terrace, 129, *130–31*, *139*; bird feeder, 138; comparisons with, *144–45*, 147; exterior, *128*, 129, *130–31*, *134*, *136–37*; plan, 129, *132–33*; guest tent, 125, *138*; influence on "Larch" house, *142–45*, 144, 147; kitchen, 129, 137; living space, 129, *130*, 135
order and complexity; *see* complex order

Pacific Northwest Ballet (PNB), 11, 57, 77, *77*, 85, 106–8, 124
Palo Alto, California, 79; Castilleja School, 85, 157n26
Pangrazio, John, 78–80
Pelli, César, 88, *88*

Pew house, 37, *37*
Pike and Virginia building, 57–61, *58, 60–61,* 69, 155
Platt, John R., 28
poetics and architecture, 9, 28, 152, 155
Polk, Willis, *78,* 78–79
Pope, Sandie (Gordon's third wife), 88, 124, 125, 127, *128, 129, 137*
Portland, Oregon: Block 136, 119, *120–21,* 123; Press Blocks, 119, *119*
Princeton Bio Center (New Jersey), 85
Pritchard, Theodore Jan, 33, 35, 86
Puget Sound School, 11, 14, 40, *41, 43, 45,* 52, 156n17, 156n21

Quigley, Rob, 82

Raff, Katherine and Douglass, 13–15, 19–20, 45, 47, 70, 76, 155. *See also* Raff house (Seattle); Raff house II
Raff house (Seattle), 13–29; AIA-Sunset Magazine Citation for, 28; children's memories of, 20, 28; comparisons with, 47, 48, 151, 155; complexity of, 152; concrete block construction, 14, 17–19, 28; contract drawings, 15, *15–16;* exterior and entry, 19, *19, 21–22, 27, 29;* Gordon as builder and general contractor for, 17; isometric drawings, *17–18;* kitchen and dining space, 15, 20, *22–26,* 28; living space, 15, 19–20, *22, 24–26,* 28; in Seattle Art Museum's Exhibition of Residential Architecture, 28; Sundberg's reaction to, 59
Raff house II (Whidbey Island), 79, *80–81,* 152
Ratti, Dean, 17
Reece, Joanne, 86, 90
Reese, Nels, 34
Reinhold, Ralph, 32
RHAA (Royston, Hanamoto, Alley, and Abey), 82, 86–87

Rodriguez, Kelly, 8, 93, 157n32
Rogers, Brent, 77, 80
Rogers, Pat and Jane, 43, 51
Rogers-Morris house, 43, *45*
Rogers house (Lopez Island): bedroom area, 101–2, *103;* comparisons with, 151; design and plans, 93–94, *100,* 101–2, 152, *173;* exterior, *98–99,* 101; kitchen and dining space, 101–2, *101–2;* living space, *101,* 101–2; paired beams in, 101–2, *103,* 152; second building, 101–2, *103;* stair and micro-library, 101–2, *102–3*
Ruskin, John, 156n11
Russell, Francia, 57, 77, 108, *171*

Saarinen, Eero, 152, 156n8
Sagle, Idaho, 32
St John Wilson, Colin, 155
Sandpoint, Idaho, 32, 34–35; *see* "Larch" house
San Francisco: Halladie Building, *78, 79;* Mithun branch in, 115; NBBJ branch in, 78–80; Sutter Street office of Walker Architecture, 85
Schell, Paul, 64, 67, 72, 76, 79–80
Schindler, Rudolf, 152
Schwabacher Hardware warehouse, *72,* 73
Seagram Building, 35, 64
Seattle, Washington: Aurora Avenue, 117, *118;* The Bakery, 52, 57, 64, 125; Century 21 Exposition, 14, 39, 85, 157n28; DeLaurenti Deli, 108; Domaine project and "Inhabit" prototype, 117, *118;* Good Shepherd Center, 57, 77; Grand Central Building, 52; Maud Building, 47, 52; Maynard Building, *52–53,* 52–54, 73; Nordic Heritage Museum, 124–25, *125;* Olmsted Plan, 86; Pike Place Market, 57–59, 108; Pike Place Market Authority, 59, 73; Pioneer Square, 40, 43, 47, 52, 73; Queen Anne Hill, 13, 117; Seattle Art Museum's

22nd Annual Exhibition, 28; Seattle Center, 57, 77, *77,* 85–86; Unico Properties, 117–19, *118*
Siegl, Terri (Gordon's second wife), 72, 75, 82
Sloan, Bill, 52
Smith, Robert, 54
Smith town houses (Seattle), 54–57, *55–57,* 79, 151, 152
Sorensen, Fleming, 54
Spokane, Washington: Cathedral of St. John the Evangelist, 34
Steinbrueck, Victor, 57–59, 73
Stickney, Jerry, 43, 156n14
Stone, Edward, 152, 156n8
Storey, Ellsworth, 88, 127, *128*
Stowell, Kent, 57, 77, *171*
Sullivan, Louis, 52, 73, 152, 157n23, 157n40
Sundberg, Rick, 52, 59, 67, 69, 73
Suyama, George, 43

Talache, Idaho, 31–32, *33,* 34, 47; Talache Resort, 37, *38*
Thiry, Paul, 85–86, 157n25, 157n28
Tonn, Roberta "Bobbie" (Gordon's first wife), 13, 14, 39–40, 43, 48, 61

Unico Properties, 117–19, *118*
Unity Temple, *36,* 36–37, 54, 152
University of California, 11; Davis campus, 151; Davis Medical Center, 80–82, *83;* Irvine campus, 151; Irvine Medical Center, 82, 90–93, *91;* Irvine student recreation center, 85; Riverside, 82; San Diego, 82, *83, 122,* 151
University of Idaho: 11, Administration Building, 88–89, 90; Albertson Hall, 86, 88, *88–89,* 90; Campus Plan, *86–87,* 86–90; Gordon as instructor at, 11, 52, 141; Gordon as student at, 32–36; Kappa Kappa Gamma sorority, 34; Lionel Hampton School of Music, 88, *88;* Campus Development Plan, 82; Olmsted's

plan for, 86, *86,* 157n29; Phi Gamma Delta fraternity, 34, *34;* ROTC, 35–36
University of Washington: 11, Applied Physics Laboratory, 75; Gordon as instructor at, 11, 141; Hugo Winkenwerder Hall, *40, 41, 43;* School of Music building, 34; Rome Studies Program, Department of Architecture, 75

van der Veen, Ron, 115

Wachsmann, Konrad, 127, 129
Waddington, house, 47, *48–49*
Wagoner, Bob, 54, 57
Walker, Colin (Gordon's son), 43, 85, 93, 108, 115, 142, 144, 157n30
Walker, Gordon: as contractor/builder, 17, 48; birth, childhood, 31–32, 156n10; compared to other architects, 152; education of, 14, 31–39; European travel (1963), 39–40; marriage to Bobbie Tonn, 13, 14, 39–40, 43, 48, 61; as fly-fishing guide, 32, 125; influence of, 116–17, 123–25; influences on, 35, 36–37, 39, 54, 152; as mentor and educator, 11, 52, 115–24, 141–47, 151; Nicholas Court home of, 93, *93;* as painter, 39; Orcas Island home of, 127–38; overview of career, 11, 48, 61, 85, 108–9, 116–17, 151; personality of, 11, 123–25, 151, 152; photographs of, *7, 114, 116–17, 122, 137, 149, 153;* Pike and Virginia Building apartment of, 59–61, *60–61,* 155; marriage to Terri Siegl, 72, 75, 82; marriage to Sandie Pope, 88, 124, *137;* timeline of career, 158–63; *For specific jobs, see name of employer, and for specific projects, see location or name of client*
Walker, Harlan (Gordon's father), 31–32, 34

Walker, Ian (Gordon's son), 72, 75
Walker, Margaret Louise (Gordon's mother), 31–32
Walker, Meagan (Gordon's daughter), 43, 149
Walker Architecture (1990–2004), 85–109; closing, 109, 115; King joining, 93; Miller (Colleen) joining, 88; move to Seattle (1992), 88, 149; Pope joining, 88; son Colin joining, 85, 157n35
Washington State University, 11?, 39
Waterfront Yacht Club (Gordon's senior project), 37–39, *38*
Whidbey Island: Langley gazebo, 80–82, *82;* Stowell-Russell house, 108, *110–13, 176;* Raff house II, 79, *80–81,* 152
Whitehouse and Price, 34, *34*
Wickersham, Albert, 52–54, 73
Winkenwerder Hall, *40, 41, 43*
Wohlert, Wilhelm, 40
Woodward, Robin, 64
Wordsworth, William, 28
Wright, Bagley, 51, 156n16
Wright, Frank Lloyd, 11, 14, 152, 156n9, 157n27; Hitchcock on, 35, 156n9; influence on Gordon, 36–37, 54; Pew house, 37, *37;* Robie house and other Chicago works of, 36; Unity Temple, *36,* 36–37, 54, 152

Yamasaki, Minoru, 157n24
Yesler Building, *73.*
YGH (Youst, Grube, Hall), 90
Youngren, Jim, 67

Zarina, Astra, 75, 76
Zevi, Bruno, 11

BIBLIOGRAPHY

Appleton, Jay, *The Experience of Landscape*. New York: Wiley, 1975. Rev. ed. 1996.

Architectural Forum. January 1938, January 1948, and June 1959.

Banister Fletcher, Sir. *A History of Architecture: On the Comparative Method for Students, Craftsmen & Amateurs.* London: B. T. Batsford, 1993.

Scribner's; editions from 1905 to the present.

Frommer, Arthur. *Europe on Five Dollars a Day.* New York: Wiley, 1957.

Herbert, Gilbert. *The Dream of the Factory-Made House: Walter Gropius and Konrad Wachsmann.* Cambridge, Mass.: MIT Press, 1984.

Hildebrand, Grant, *The Wright Space: Pattern and Meaning in Frank Lloyd Wright's Houses.* Seattle: University of Washington Press, 1991.

———. *Origins of Architectural Pleasure.* Berkeley: University of California Press, 1999.

———, and T. William Booth. *A Thriving Modernism: The Houses of Wendell Lovett and Anny Bystrom.* Seattle: University of Washington Press, 2004.

Hitchcock, Henry-Russell. *In the Nature of Materials, 1887–1941: The Buildings of Frank Lloyd Wright.* New York: Da Capo Press, 1942.

Johnston, Norman J. *University of Washington: The Campus Guide.* New York: Princeton Architectural Press, 2001.

Kellert, Stephen, Judi Heerwagen, and Martin Mador. *Biophilic Design: The Theory, Science, and Practice of Bringing Buildings to Life.* New York: Wiley, 2008.

Seattle Homes and Lifestyles for August of 2002.

Sunset Magazine, October 1971.

Wright, Frank Lloyd. *An Autobiography.* London: Longmans, Green & Co., 1932.

———. *A Testament.* New York: Bramhall House, 1957.

Zevi, Bruno. *Architecture as Space: How to Look at Architecture.* New York: Da Capo Press, 1993.

AUTHOR
BIOGRAPHY

FOLLOWING A PROFESSIONAL DEGREE IN ARCHITECTURE from the University of Michigan in 1957, and professional practice with Minoru Yamasaki and Albert Kahn in1964, Grant Hildebrand completed the master's program in architecture at Michigan and began a teaching career at the University of Washington. In 1974 his book, *Designing for Industry: The Architecture of Albert Kahn*, was published by MIT Press. The following year he received the University's Distinguished Teaching Award for the rank of professor.

In 1978 he became interested in the work of Jay Appleton, who argued that the appeal of certain landscapes is based in part on the survival advantages they offer. In 1988 Hildebrand inaugurated a course in the architectural implications of such an approach. This led to the publication of *The Wright Space: Pattern and Meaning in Frank Lloyd Wright's Houses* by UW Press in 1991. Hildebrand expanded this toward a general aesthetic theory in *Origins of Architectural Pleasure*, published by the University of California Press in 1999, for which he received the Washington Governor's Writers' Award for work of literary merit and lasting value.

Professor Hildebrand was Chettle Fellow at the University of Sydney, Australia, in 1989, and has held visiting appointments at Tokyo Institute of Technology and the Universities of Pennsylvania, Michigan, and Oregon. He retired from teaching in 2000 and he continues to write. In 2004 he coauthored with T. William Booth *A Thriving Modernism: The Houses of Wendell Lovett and Arne Bystrom*, which was short-listed for the Washington Governor's Writers' Award, and in 2007 he published *Frank Lloyd Wright's Palmer House* and *Elegant Explorations: The Designs of Phillip Jacobson*. In the same year he and his wife, Miriam, self-published *A Greek Temple in French Prairie*, the story of the pre-Civil War William Case house in the Willamette Valley of Oregon. *Suyama: A Complex Serenity* and its companion, *Gene Zema: Architect, Craftsman,* were published by UW Press and Marquand Tieton in 2011. Hildebrand also self-published an anthology of his poems, *Autumn Leaves: Poems 2004–2012*, which has received no awards whatsoever.

Library of Congress Control Number: 2019932574
ISBN 978-1-7328214-0-8

Published by ARCADE, Seattle
www.arcadenw.org

Distributed by University of Washington Press
www.washington.edu/uwpress

Produced by Lucia|Marquand, Seattle
www.luciamarquand.com

Edited by Ellen Wheat
Designed by Ryan Polich
Typeset in Whitney by Maggie Lee
Proofread by Laura Lesswing
Indexed by Enid Zafran
Color management by iocolor, Seattle
Printed and bound in China by Artron Art Group

With great appreciation for donors to this project:

Jane and Bob Brahm
Emanuela Frattini and Carl Magnusson
Philip Jacobson
J.A.S. Design Build
Johnston Hastings Grant
Floyd Udell Jones
Douglas Kelbaugh
Dave Miller
Mithun
Alene Moris
Abigail and Scott Morris
Jeffrey Murdock and Mathew Albores
Olson Kundig
Katherine and Douglass Raff
Victoria Reed
Francia Russell and Kent Stowell
Gene Zema

Page 7: Photograph by Zhenru Zhang
Page 153: Photograph by Juan Hernandez

meadow   slope   meadow